Donut Holes for the Soul

Recollections, Musings, and Missives
from the Dooryard

Timothy Cotton

CAMDEN, MAINE
ESSEX, CONNECTICUT

Down East Books

An imprint of The Globe Pequot Publishing Group, Inc.
64 South Main Street
Essex, CT 06426
www.globepequot.com

Distributed by NATIONAL BOOK NETWORK

British Library Cataloguing in Publication Information available

Library of Congress Cataloging-in-Publication Data

Names: Cotton, Timothy (Detective), author.
Title: Donut holes for the soul : recollections, musings, and missives from the dooryard / Timothy Cotton.
Description: Camden, Maine : Down East Books, 2025.
Identifiers: LCCN 2025002804 (print) | LCCN 2025002805 (ebook) | ISBN 9781684752485 (cloth) | ISBN 9781684752775 (epub)
Subjects: LCGFT: Essays.
Classification: LCC PS3603.O86947 D66 2025 (print) | LCC PS3603.O86947 (ebook) | DDC 814/.6—dc23/eng/20250207
LC record available at https://lccn.loc.gov/2025002804
LC ebook record available at https://lccn.loc.gov/2025002805

∞™ The paper used in this publication meets the minimum requirements of American National Standard for Information Sciences—Permanence of Paper for Printed Library Materials, ANSI/NISO Z39.48-1992.

Contents

Contents

Contents

The Ears Have It

Thwap, thwap, thwap, thwap, thwap—never another, always with the five thwaps. It's a reset to stop the clinging. With her head shaking and ears readjusting, Ellie is like a lady fluffing out her skirt after being seated too long in a church service.

After compressing her ear flaps into a crevice near the arm of the couch, the leather loveseat, or any other of her chosen nighttime venues, fluffing of the ears is necessary. When she gets up, the only sound is the click of her claws on the hardwood floors or of the soft threads as she rakes her paws across the living room rug. First, she stretches, sometimes yawning. Then comes the obligatory stroll down the hall. She goes into full thwapping mode about three strides before getting to my bedroom door. It's loud, and it almost sounds painful—the resetting of the ears.

Then, like a mother checking on her child, she stands in my doorway—backlit by a nightlight down the hall—hopeful that the thwapping has brought me around to consider a trip outside and a chaser of kibble and fresh water. Then it's my turn. If I want ten more minutes of rest, I have a standard slogan, "It's time to lie down." But if I say, "Good morning, Ellie," that starts the tail; once that kicks off, there is no stopping it.

If I ask her to lie down, she walks to her soft bed over by the closet and thumps down, huffing out an exasperated groan fueled by minor joint pain and frustration that all the drama was for naught.

I have to give her credit; that's all I have to say to get a little more sleep. She makes no other noises unless I stay in bed too long and she happens to catch a glimpse of the sunrise in one of the bedroom windows. But I rarely make her wait until the sun shows up. I typically only need a few minutes to contemplate what a waste of time it is to stay in bed past a quarter of four.

Thwap, thwap, thwap, thwap, thwap—never another, always with the five thwaps.

If she can rise, I can, too. It's the shining that takes effort.

THE MUNDANE—
REFLECTIONS FROM SOUTH DAKOTA

I'M SPOILED. I'VE SEEN MUCH OF THE COUNTRY ON SOMEONE else's dime, but it very well could have been yours. If so, I thank all of you.

I've been to Sioux Falls, South Dakota, thrice within a month and a half—and I've enjoyed every visit. I found the people genuine and the scenery breathtaking (for a kid from the Jagged Edge of America). I loved that the folks there could register an all-terrain vehicle for road use.

Yeah, I found that out when a Honda Rubicon ATV passed me on I-90 while we were driving to lunch at a place that claimed to have foot-long hot dogs. They did, by the way, and they were good.

You see, I am not an accidental tourist. Since I was always working on my business trips, I made sure that I saw things that most people would find mundane. Mundane is open all the time. Life—to Timmy—is cobbled together, secured by the mundane.

I visited the South Dakota Battleship Memorial in the center of Sioux Falls. Silly me, being from a maritime state, I thought I'd see the entire ship. I was wrong. It was the outline of the boat in a park. I had to use my imagination.

Volunteers run the tiny museum there. They can picture the ship because they must; it's not there. The spirit of the battlewagon lives a proud and vibrant life, and the South Dakota people honor her and the sailors who crewed the ship. Necessity is the mother of invention and the crazy uncle of imagination. It's a fantastic spot, respectfully done. I appreciate that.

On the one day that our murder suspect was unable to speak with us we made our way to Devil's Gulch. It's up near Garrettson. Jesse James is said to have jumped the gulch when on horseback, apparently running full speed, fleeing a bank robbery in nearby (as the crow flies) Minnesota. James jumped the 18-foot-wide chasm in 1876; there is no video. I used my imagination again. There are some naysayers.

Volunteers also staff a replica western-themed cabin near the launch site. The day my partner and I were there, killing time until our suspect could be fed lunch at the Minnehaha County Jail, we met a pleasant gentleman who shared some of the suspicions held by locals concerning whether Jesse James indeed jumped the gorge on a horse. We appreciated his honesty.

Myself, I believe it. I must. I must believe, for I have been there. I've been to a lot of other places, usually because the murder suspects got there first while trying to avoid speaking to me or another cop or two. Missoula, Montana; Baltimore, Maryland; Spokane, Washington (one suspected killer wouldn't stay put, so we followed him around for a few days; eating the perfect steak in northern Idaho made the trip worthwhile).

On our final trip across South Dakota, we were getting tired and thirsty from the seven-hundred-mile day of driving. With the sun at our backs, we hurriedly drove from Rapid City toward our hotel in Sioux Falls. We were in awe as we drove, watching the vast fields being scoured clean by huge combines, something two simple cops from the Jagged Edge had never seen. We both were impressed with how many of those combines sported a very proud waving American flag. No one was burning them there, I can assure you.

We'd been near Wyoming and had done a few witness interviews, taking a quick visit to Mt. Rushmore and the Crazy Horse memorial between conversing with humans who, in part, were lying to us about our suspect's past. We were used to that part of the job. None cared that they were being watched ever so carefully by honest Abe or the notoriously honest George Washington.

We pulled off at a nondescript exit for fuel and cheap snacks. Rolling to a stop just off the exit, we ended up on a gravel farm road infested by dusty, rust-less pickup trucks (they were well-used working trucks, but no rust), some without tailgates. At the store, maybe a mile from I-90, we didn't fit in, because we weren't dusty or sore.

The thing I remember most was how cordial everyone was. It was clear we weren't locals; we wore ties. Oh, they were loosely hanging from our necks, but they were ties nonetheless, hovering over dress slacks and formerly shiny shoes. We'd locked our guns in the glovebox, figuring we were safe from malfeasant ne'er-do-wells. We didn't need no stinking badges.

I talked with a ballcap-wearing farmer who didn't even ask what we were doing there. He looked tired and worn out, but we chatted; I asked questions about how long the harvest would last. He smiled after explaining so an idiot could understand, then said, "Have a safe trip," knowing that I didn't belong but offering hope for no problems on the way to where I was going.

Outside, my partner finished filling the gas tank. He looked at me and said, "I like it here." I stood in the dust-filled breeze and strongly agreed, passing him water and a portion of beef jerky. I said, "I think I'd like living here," knowing I never would.

Why do I write about this? I can't tell you, except that it's mundane yet memorable.

That's why traveling, no matter the reason, is essential: to see life, even a glimmer of it, outside the place where you are most comfortable.

In the years since those trips to the breadbasket of America, my partner and I have often waxed profound about that trip and the ensuing journey driving a now-convicted, since-freed, man across America in a minivan. That's a story in itself.

And, yes, he and I disagree about whether Jesse jumped the gorge and whether there's a better way to represent a storied battleship without water to float the hull. But we both loved the hot dogs.

It's the mundane that makes our time here worth re-membering. Keep it in mind.

Keep the Change If You Can Find It

According to the notification's heading, I'm approved for another credit card, which has had no impact on my credit score—they are so good to me. It's the fifth one this week: two by mail and three by email. When a credit card carrier sends you five unrequested blank checks begging you to run up your balance, you have to wonder how their collections department can keep up with the onslaught of bad decisions. Not everyone has self-control. If I am getting these, I surmise there is something similar in every mailbox in the country.

Each time I tear up an offer, I become a tad paranoid and tear it into even smaller pieces. I imagine a malfeasant puzzle specialist finding the contents of the trash bin and methodically putting the checks back together, then buying a new Corvette or a PlayStation; it all depends on whether the thief is wearing sneakers from New Balance or a pair of Jordans—IYKYK.

As if it matters, I sometimes transfer a few pieces to separate bins, hopefully demanding they be good at scavenger hunts, too. My mother runs bulk mail through a shredder in case some innocuous detail can be gleaned, enabling someone to clean out her bank account. But she's a puzzle specialist.

However, she is also a patient practitioner—the most dangerous type of criminal mind. I found out how good she was during her recent move. Sitting in her recliner sipping a pre-packing coffee, I noticed a folded twenty-dollar bill on the side table. I picked it up and hailed her to put it in her purse so she wouldn't lose track of it during the loading process. She spoke from the other room, "It's no good; I found it in a box. It's one that Dudley ate years ago while Dad was pastoring the church in Portland."

Only when I unfolded the bill did I discover that Dudley, a massive, happy golden retriever—long passed—was crafty enough to chew off much of the serial number from Andrew Jackson's favorite folding money. Mom relayed that "The Dud" had eaten four twenties—eighty bucks—taken from a tabletop while they were next door at the church one Sunday. "That's the only one that I couldn't save. The bank said there wasn't enough of the number to be able to replace it." "What about the other three, Mother?" I said.

My mother came along right after the Great Depression, "Oh, I followed him around the backyard for two days, collected the pieces, and put them back together. I even found some on the third day. That was the only almost complete bill." "The bank took all those #$it covered bills?" I laughed. "Timothy, watch your language." I stopped laughing.

"Of course, I washed them all. And I used gloves during the collection. I had to tape them together." "Did you bleach them?" "Of course I did. Then, I taped them together. It took me a while. It was years ago." "Mom, I have to give you credit. Not many people would have the fortitude or patience to do this."

I stared at the bill in my hand, knowing where it had traveled, unbothered because I knew that my mother's idea of clean and mine were vastly different. She uses bleach in defiance of all the silly rules of engagement.

"So, you took three taped twenties to the bank, and they gave you back three pristine bills?"

"Yes."

"And this one is the one that they rejected?"

"Yes, the others were chewed up in smaller pieces, but I found all the numbers, so they were acceptable for exchange."

"Mother, you are the reason I tear up my mail and put it in separate containers at the post office."

All I am trying to tell you is—if you have a dog—place your bills up high when you head to church. If you don't, I know a lady.

SLEEVES

I'd MANAGED TO KEEP THE WELL OF TEARS HIDDEN, NOT quite prepared to share it. Like anyone working through grief, it can overwhelm your stoic nature without fair warning.

In the last few weeks, along with my little sister, I have been focusing on moving my Mama to her new island home. Mom has moved twice over the last couple of years, first from a large apartment at my home and now from the smaller place where she shared the last days with my dad, her husband of sixty-six years. We hoped the simplicity of the living arrangement would help him thrive longer, but we don't control those things, do we?

I've sensed some frustration from Mom, as she doesn't like being told what to do, and sometimes, I can be short and to the point. As her son, I assure you that I do it out of love. This move has been challenging and overwhelming, forcing her to focus on getting rid of more of her lifetime of memories and possessions. It can be paralyzing, and it makes me deeply sorrowful to have to oversee it all. Moving her into a single, large bedroom demands that we make hard choices.

One of my toughest moments came yesterday while I was leaning over a moving dolly, wiping away sweat while taking a break from loading yet another trunkful of her life into her little car, trying to make sure that she made it to the coast in time to get onto the three o'clock ferry boat. Out of the blue, she said, "I can't get over how much you look like your Daddy." I had to turn away, focusing on the sunshine coming through the window, hoping the bright light in my eyes could be blamed for the welling up of tears. But she knew. You can't hide your feelings from your Mama.

I hustled another load down the hall, out the doors, and into her little blue Honda. While outside, I took an extra minute to dry the inevitable leakage onto the sleeve of my flannel. I don't control those things, you know?

Once I had her buckled in the car and crushed down the excessive dunnage in the backseat so that she could peek at cars behind her in the rearview, I kissed her head and told her to call when she was in line for the ferry boat. "Do you have a book, in case you're there early?" "No, but I'll be fine. Don't forget to tell the ladies in the kitchen that I won't be down to the dining room tonight for supper; I told them I was coming." "I'll take care of it. How much gas do you have?" "Over half a tank." "You can stop for gas, but they also have gas on the island. You have plenty to get there. Just don't miss the boat. Maybe Jason can come across the bay and pick you up if you do, or I'll drive down to grab you, and you can stay at my house tonight." She laughed. "I'm not helpless, you know." "I know that, Mama. I know that."

I watched her leave, surprised at her caution behind the wheel, feeling bad for anyone behind her who might be in a hurry. I finished moving more items and cleaning up the place a bit more, then headed home. It was late in the day when I saw a round rainbow orb on my cupboard—it had never happened before, but that's a story about yesterday.

Today, my nephew drove up from southern Maine. He moved into his first house with his family, and there were some furnishings that we had that he could use. He came to my Mom and Dad's old apartment at the far end of my house, where some of their old furniture still resides. We loaded the truck quickly since we had to pick up a few extra things from Mom's now-old apartment.

Mom had lost a special ring years ago, her Mother's Ring; she's been sad about it, but she never complains; she hides her tears like I do.

What you need to know about my mom is that her kids have always been the most important people in her life. She never worked outside the home, simply so she could be there when we left and when we got home. She made our meals, kissed our boo-boos, and told me—often—to go to my room to wait for my father to get home.

My siblings and I bought her a four-stone Mother's Ring a long, long time ago. One day, she lost it, never complaining but sadly and quietly longing to get it back. So much so that we, her kids, bought her another last year. She loves it, but it's different from the original. It's not the one she got on Mother's Day when we first surprised her. Dad was here then, too.

My nephew and I were moving furniture into the box truck that afternoon. Mom had to leave many furnishings behind the first time she and Daddy moved away—furniture they'd had for thirty years, maybe longer. I've kept their apartment empty except for their excess belongings, mostly because I can't find it in my heart to rent the space. I've had more than my fair share of frustration in dealing with people's problems, and I am not accepting or importing new issues at this point in life. It's simply cold storage. My Dad's bedroom looks almost exactly like it did when he left, and I like it that way.

Hastily, I emptied some drawers on a small occasional table that had been close to my mother's recliner for decades—pens, papers, notes to self, a tape measure, lifesavers, and pennies. I even found some forever postage stamps, and I felt good that I could give them to her the next time I saw her. After loading was complete, I returned to the main apartment door, waiting to go through and see if there was anything else my nephew needed.

I looked down and noticed a glimmer of gold. I knew what it was immediately. We have had many discussions centering on her sadness at losing the prized possession. It must have fallen out of that chairside stand. However, I had emptied the single drawer in its entirety into a small plastic trash can, and I was thorough, even in my haste. Once I pointed the treasure out to my nephew, I said, "That ring has been missing for years. It could have fallen out anywhere outside in the driveway and rolled under the leaves or into the mud, but it fell right on this rug in the doorway. It's like somebody placed it there." Scotty said, "Wow, Uncle, talk about a God thing."

I looked for a beam of sunlight, hoping I could blame the tears on something else, but I gave up and used my sleeve again. I called my mother. She was in the kitchen at my sister's. I relayed the story in short, supposing she might have taken it off to put lotion on her hands at some point, placed it safely in a drawer, and forgotten where she stored it. It could also have been stuck in a crevice of that table; neither of us knew, but her original Mother's Ring would be back on her finger within a week or so.

For a few moments, Mom's voice sounded different, better.

She shed tears and had a slight quiver in her voice. She was amazed and thankful. A heartfelt ensemble of sheer delight accompanied all of that.

It was raining, and since I was alone in my truck, I went directly for my sleeve again. But we don't control those things, do we?

Looking Forward to Something

During my first nineteen years of life, we moved seventeen times; I know the figure is correct, but memory serves me poorly sometimes. If I sat down with pen and paper, I could sketch out a timeline for you, but I'll spare you the details. Most often, we were within the boundaries of Maine, but Dad threw us a curve in the summer before my senior year in high school—"What do you think about living in Georgia for a while?"

I didn't think much of it at all. I didn't argue, but I recall moping around after he finalized the decision. I was accustomed to loading and unloading furniture up and down the ramps of rented moving vans, so that part was second nature.

He'd taken a pastorship at a small northern Georgia church and was going to work on his theological degree at a college there. He forged ahead with the plan, buying a small brick ranch on a quiet street. The house had central air conditioning, something unheard of in Maine but necessary for a houseful of Yankees hanging around in the hot south.

I was to finish my senior year of high school there, and I was terrified about it. The school was huge, and I was used to being in a small school in a small town. I remember the first time Dad drove me by the behemoth; it looked like a shopping mall compared to any school I'd ever attended.

Maine to Georgia in the cab of a U-Haul is a long poke. I was seventeen, so our conversations on that ride were some of our most important. In comparison to earlier, shorter rides, it was an epic adventure.

By June 1980, U-Haul box trucks, usually Fords, had AM radios installed in the dash, but you barely could hear them over the roar of the giant gas engine, especially with the windows rolled down.

I remember a lot of Billy Joel songs—and top-forty fodder, such as Robbie Dupree, Ambrosia, and Tom Petty. You get the idea. Rupert Holmes had already charted and wore out our eardrums with "Escape," but "Him"—a hit that summer—solidified Holmes as a master songwriter in my seventeen-year-old mind. I have always enjoyed trying to copy his subtle, melodic understatement and include some of that spirit in my writing. Whether I'm successful is another story. But Holmes was. Agree with me or don't; that man is a master wordsmith.

I didn't smoke, but I can't tell you how many times I sang out the truck's open window, "Over by the window, there's a pack of cigarettes, not my brand, you understand; sometimes a girl forgets." The words flowed so well together, fitting like pieces of a puzzle. I loved the way Holmes transitioned that piece from a feeling that there was forgetfulness, slipping into the most sinister, "She forgets to hide them, I know who left those smokes behind, She'll say, 'ah, he's just a friend,' and I'll say, 'Oh, I'm not blind.'" I digress.

Dad let me control the radio dial on that trip. But now and then, he'd turn it down on secondary roads and pontificate about this or that. Usually, the only time the engine wasn't roaring was on slower roads, so he took those opportunities.

"What do you think you'll do after high school?" "I dunno, Pop. I really don't. I was thinking about being a disc jockey." "There's not much of a future in that, and probably only a few openings. Whatever you do, do your best," he'd say. "Even if it's being a garbage truck driver, as you used to tell us. Be the best one ever."

And I did have that dream for a long time. I wanted to be just like the guy who picked up our trash. He'd often get out of the truck, grab one of our bicycles, and show us how to ride it around the yard—backward. It was impressive. I saw sanitation as being a doorway to that kind of skill. He was a lovely man.

I'd turn up the radio after Dad finished, giving it enough time to ensure we would not have to turn it down again for a more in-depth conversation. Often, we stopped for some cold sodas and Slim Jims. My mother and sister were close behind in the blue Impala station wagon. Somewhere, maybe in Virginia, but I'm not sure, he gave me a piece of advice I've clung to forever. Well, at least since 1980. It was a time when I didn't believe I'd ever see old age, the death of my dad, the sadnesses of life, a successful short career in radio—my dad used to listen to my show—and a long career as a cop.

"Timmy, one thing is for sure: you have to have fun in life. The Lord expects us to have fun. He gave us so much on earth to enjoy, and we should, you know? You need to look out ahead. Keep in mind that you should have long-term goals. That's all well and good. But make sure you plan to do something fun, even if it's months or years away. Then, make sure you do it." I understood him.

Some people, even him, have accused me of not taking everything as seriously as I should. But Dad understood me. We laughed at a lot of things together.

His follow-up, a synopsis of that conversation, came a few years before I married. "Plan something special—something fun. When you wake up every day to the monotony of life and work, you both will still have something to look forward to down the road. It's important. It makes life on earth worth living, and there's something better coming anyway." Dad had a way of preaching to you without slamming the book on the pulpit.

In an age when suicide is in every news feed, I can't help but think how my dad's simple advice could help a whole lot of humans, even to get just one more day. To have something, anything, to look forward to would save lives. Instill that thought in your kids, and then show them how.

I know many people are in pain, but believing something better is somewhere down the road has always been helpful to me. Dad told me so, and he was right.

We need to keep in mind that there are things to look forward to. It's a powerful concept.

THE QUALITIES OF THE DRAPE

I PICKED OUT THREE SHIRTS THAT BELONGED TO MY OLD Man. I took them from the closet with permission from my mom, who had taken an out-of-town break after Dad passed away. Some of his shirts fit me well, some not so much.

As expected, I went through the pockets—his pockets. He might have left me a few bucks for a coffee, which would have tasted pretty good right about then. He didn't, but I could picture him smiling because he would have gone through the pockets as well.

I unwrapped the lone Hall's cough drop from the left shirt pocket of his long-sleeved heather green houndstooth flannel and let it dissolve in my mouth on the way home in the truck. It's a dressy flannel, and I don't have any. Mine are plaids, usually blocky, always the same as all the other guys who wear the same brand as me. Men don't care if we buy the same shirt as another guy. You might even glance over and give them a subtle nod at the pub or the hardware store, noting that it most likely was purchased during the end-of-winter sale before Carhartt released the new patterns. "Ah, another value shopper. Good for you."

Flannels are not one-off prom dresses; they're shirts meant to be removed and tossed over the hood of the pickup if the sun gets too warm when you help your neighbor load an old couch or folded up and set on the ground to protect your old knees from pebbles when you get under the truck to find out what's rattling at fifty-one miles per hour, but only when you let off the gas pedal.

Dad found some shirt sleeves too long for him, but I found them just about right for me. However, I kept them rolled up because he did. It's one thing to skim him for coffee; it's another to defile the qualities of the drape—at least for now.

My mom called me the other day to see if I wanted more shirts. I told her I'd picked out three, and that was all I could handle. I can't tell you why that is. I don't know. There's a lot I don't know.

I know it's okay to call him my Old Man because he was. It wouldn't have been an option when I was fifteen. That would have invited minor deserved violence, I say. His shirts would have been too big then, anyway.

As life progressed, he used the term with me in phone messages, usually if I was three minutes late to pick him up for our breakfasts out on the town. "Hey, Tim. This is the Old Man. Did you say eight-thirty?" His passive aggressiveness was some of the kindest I have ever had to put up with. It was indeed a question, not a judgment.

I'd listen to those messages after breakfast on my way home from dropping him off and laugh to myself. "I was only three minutes late," I'd mumble. I mostly keep my ringer off, so I missed the calls, and he'd never mention that he had called me just before I pulled in to pick him up. He had little patience for tardiness. Eight-thirty to my Old Man meant eight-fifteen sharp.

I wore the one with a faux fleece lining the other day when it was cold enough. It had handwarmer pockets, and

I have to admit they were pretty handy. I rechecked the pockets as if he might have slipped me a couple of bucks for coffee. It wasn't there.

Instead, I found a pristine wad of folded Kleenex. He knew what I needed.

Orlando Frati—I Will Miss One of Bangor's Best

Whenever I encounter a perception that is not reality, I tuck it away. I'll use that in a story someday, I say to myself.

I've had this one under my hat for well over forty years. It's too bad I can only share now that not all pawnbrokers are cut from the same cloth.

Sure, most of my experience with pawnshops came from those seedy shops seen in the 1970s detective shows like *Kojak* and *Starsky and Hutch*. Those were dark places with a sweaty man behind the counter, always with a wink and a nod to the fact that somebody stole the item in question during a burglary.

Well, I have good friends in the pawn business. I must replace the words seedy and dark with one word that might appear misplaced: compassion. You see, my friend, 92-year-old Bangor Jeweler/Pawnbroker Orlando Frati, passed away recently. But it will be more than family and friends who will miss him.

I bought my first chainsaw from Mr. Frati. I couldn't afford a new saw, not for a minute. He found one for me and knew the previous owner—a regular at the shop. I cut no less than twenty cords of tree-length wood with that saw, and it already had plenty of miles on it before I picked it up for half price. I was just a kid with an old house and two woodstoves; he let me pay it off in four installments, taking it home to cut wood before I came close to paying it off. He knew a radio disc jockey didn't make enough to pay it off in one payment, and it was getting cold outside. He didn't charge me any interest, by the way.

Many do not know, and cannot picture, that a pawnbroker is a lender of last resort for many who have never darkened the door of a bank. They'd be turned away before a pull of their credit report. For a long time, it was a necessary cog in the wheel of slow financial progress. In the days of yore, when someone needed a few bucks to pay the mortgage, there was no Facebook Marketplace to sell the kitchen mixer or the old golf clubs in the basement. They went to and trusted their local pawnbroker.

If you have a more positive view of banks over most of these local neighborhood lenders, you are a product of good advertising polished only by the sight of shiny shoes topped off by a cheap suit from Penney's. You could be tainted, like I was, by watching *Kojak*.

Never have I seen a banker tell a customer that it was okay to pay their loan off next month—longer if it helped, along with, "I hope your husband feels better soon." I have seen Mr. Frati and his son do that on multiple occasions, sometimes knowing that the person lied about why they couldn't pay their bill and pick up their pawned item. It didn't matter. I've heard Orlando senior say, "They'll be back," knowing they merely needed a little more time.

Orlando Frati's pawnshop on State Street in Bangor, Maine, has been a staple for over a century; you only last that long with integrity and a conscience. Regular customers, sometimes down on their luck, have entrusted them with holding and securing their treasured belongings, heirlooms, watches, and—sometimes—kitchen appliances until their financial outlook improved.

Later in life, as a cop, I received many phone calls from the Frati men about someone coming to the shop trying to sell something that really "didn't seem right." I solved multiple burglaries before they were reported due to the diligence of the Fratis. Knowing the difference between a customer needing a little more time and a miscreant trying to sell off his alleged "grandfather's gun collection" takes someone who knows their customer base.

Long before it was a city ordinance for local re-sellers to report the items they purchased each month, Mr. Frati would walk his handwritten list to the police department, dropping it at the counter for the detectives to see, "just in case."

When his business came under far more scrutiny and regulation than antique shops, video stores, and some big-box sellers who could buy from customers with zero oversight, he brought his list to the station, knowing that many items that he used to buy were being sold surreptitiously to others who did not fall under the pawnbroker ordinances. Ordinances were based mainly on the belief that only licensed pawnbrokers dealt with stolen merchandise. It's just not true. I'll attest to all of it.

Beyond his compassion for his customers and friends, Mr. Orlando Frati was a lovely man with a love for his family and a work ethic that no longer exists in society. A veteran of the Korean conflict, he was only gone from the shop for a couple of years to fight a war. He came back with a different outlook on the world but continued treating his customers with respect, some down and out because of life's downturns, some because of continuous bad choices. I never saw the latter treated any differently.

He was still coming to the shop well into his 92nd year. He'd always offer me a doughnut. "Tim, it looks like you're losing weight," he'd say, smiling in the wry way that indicated that he noted I'd gained far more than ten pounds. He was there every day, cracking jokes, making people smile, and still loaning money on stuff that would never sell if the customer didn't return to pick it up.

So, you go ahead and trust your banker; they probably have a degree and a Mercedes. I've met some good ones. But, if I am down on my luck and have no business in a bank, I'll go where friendship is earned, and trust is freely given, even if you can't get it all paid off by next month. "They'll be back; I've known them for years." Orlando Frati meant it, and he will be missed in the City of Bangor.

Rest in peace, Mr. Frati; I'll miss you, my friend.

Santa Was on My Roof

While sweeping the back deck, I noted several shards of broken concrete. Leaves and pine needles were the focus of my attack. The windstorm left plenty. Yesterday, I picked up tree branches; today, I took on clearing out the detritus from the driveway and the decks. Merely minutes after marveling that I had never lost a shingle, I discovered the shards. Naturally, perplexed by the discovery, I picked up a chunk and examined it closely. I do believe I scratched my head.

"Concrete?" I said it out loud. Ellie's ears perked up momentarily, probably wondering if I might have said, "Come for a treat." I am not currently taking applications for new enemies, so I couldn't imagine someone throwing concrete at the house. I looked up to the roof, the only possibility, as my deck was six feet above the ground.

One side of the piece was flat and finished, the other rough. It took about ten seconds to determine that the pieces came from the chimney. The crown or cap on my chimney was clearly the source of my amalgamated displeasure, and I try to avoid roof work. Knowing that if the entire cap was found to be cracked, it meant that I would be dealing with water intrusion shortly—winter is here.

I called my good friend, Bubba. His name is not Bubba, nor does he look like one. He's a retired cop who was the master roofer responsible for my perfectly pristine shingles in the face of seventy-mile-an-hour winds. His close friends merely call him Bubba, but his name is Bob. I dialed him up while standing with the shard in my hand. He answered on the second ring. "TC, baby, what can Bubba do for you?"

"I found concrete on my deck, Bubba. I worry that the cap on my chimney is cracked, and the wind likely took off bigger pieces, but I'm holding a decent-sized chunk in my hand."

"That's not good, TC. I'm on a roof in Bangor, but I'm almost done. I'll be down in an hour."

"Thanks, Bubba. I just want to avoid water in the walls. Maybe you can seal it off for the winter."

"See you soon."

Forty-five minutes later, my phone rang, "TC, I'm in the backyard; meet me on the deck." Bob was already passing a ladder up and over the rail. "Stand on the bottom of that ladder, TC." And with that, he shot up to the roof and stood beside my chimney ten seconds later. "There's a little ice on the shingles; catch me if I come down." I watched him run his hand across the topping on the chimney.

"You are correct, young man; there is some slight cracking with some scale missing. Probably what you have in your hand. I think I did this crown, didn't I?"

"You did, Bubba, a long time ago."

"It's all good for now. I'll be down in the spring, and we can chop out the loose stuff and tighten it all up. It'll hold fine till then." Bubba came down the ladder as fast as he'd gone up. He had two more roofs to work on today. We took a few minutes to talk about the old days, his son, my son, and a few other things.

As usual, he refused to take any payment. I do know that Bubba Bait is old-school Budweiser—in bottles. I'll leave a case on his doorstep soon. He's the one who calls it "Bubba

Bait." Those of us blessed with his friendship know the only way we can repay him is to leave him a beer and run before he throws it back in our car.

The better news about his skillset is that Bubba was one of the finest cops to wear the uniform. If he's your friend, he is a friend for life and won't put up with anyone bad-mouthing you. People find that out quickly when they speak out of turn.

If you were a kid with less than much on Bubba's police beat—typically on the east side of Bangor—he'd watch out for you. I cannot count on two hands the number of new guitars and stingray bicycles that Bubba delivered to parents who didn't have anything to give to their kids on one Christmas or another. The thing is, Bubba secretly delivered the gifts to the parents so that they could give them to their children. He wanted no part of being noticed for what he was up to.

A lot of us noticed. We also learned not to bring it up to him. His gift was to help other people help their kids when times were tough, wanting nothing in return, not even a "thank you" from the child. Frankly, I don't know many people who personify selflessness like Bubba. I've met many people in my sixty trips around the sun.

An old quote says, "A gift should not flatter the giver." I think of that every time I see Bubba. He transferred his kindness to others so they could feel as special as the kid playing the guitar or riding a bike. And all along, those kids thought that Dad or Mom, or Santa, brought it to them. The rest of us knew, and we kept our mouths shut.

Santa was on my roof today. And it's highly likely that he's already on someone else's roof as we speak.

If you celebrate any one of the many national holidays in December, do it well. I'm a celebrator of Christmas—and if you are I hope it's merry and bright.

Be safe, be kind, but most of all, be you; you are perfect enough. I think the creator had a plan for all of us. If you think I'm wrong, we will still get along just fine.

Reflections from a Smoothly Swinging Door

Each time I enter the house from the back deck, it crosses my mind. I perform the task at least six or seven times daily; it's Ellie's portal to the potty.

It's not a fancy door. It's functional, swings well, and closes tightly. I participated in the installation. Oh, I've installed doors before, a couple all by my lonesome. But that was during the new construction phase at the camp in the woods—nearly thirty years ago.

Installing-the-door-when-it's-new construction is pretty simple, as long as all is level and plumb. I had a lot of help when I built the camp in the woods. The guys from work dropped everything to close it in before winter set in. That's why it was level and plumb in the first place.

I have great friends. Some, even, that I have lost track of since the cabin went up. But this is about my door. Well, two doors.

I'd been swinging an unsound door for years; it was French. Technically, it was only half French—a single door. The glass-paned egress was plumb worn out. I called Larry. I left a message because he never picks up.

"Larry, I don't need you to be here when I install the new door, but I need to know you are in the area in case I run into trouble. I'm not much of a carpenter."

Three minutes later, my phone rang. "Let me grab some tools, and I'll come down. See you in twenty."

The removal of the old door was typical of Larry. After the reciprocating saw detached the fasteners by abrasive force, he yelled, "Grab it right there and yank while I push. Put your purse down."

With some finagling, we got the door in, caulked, and put up the outer trim, and I installed the hardware. It now swings like Sammy Sosa.

I bought Larry's breakfast the following week. That's all he wanted: sausage and eggs, home fries, coffee. If I had found a tradesman, and they bothered to call back and show up, it would have cost me five hundred bucks. Larry looked like he made five hundred bucks as he dipped his buttered toast into the yolk. I feigned disgust at the cost but paid the tip, too.

Since that day, we enter with a light push every time I come back from the yard, across the deck, and into the house. There is nary a struggle. Ellie can nudge it open with her muzzle when I'm not quick enough to allow her entry. I have since put up a storm door; it truly sealed the deal.

I can holler through the summer screen for Ellie to "get back here" when she sneaks off as I refill her water bowl at the kitchen sink. I sometimes yell out the door, even when I can't see her, before she attempts to sneak off to chase the squirrels, merely to let her know I might be watching.

It's such a minor thing—the door. When I swing it, I remember the colloquy between Larry and me. I recall going to the shed searching for a thirty-six-inch piece of pressure treated two-by-four as Larry thought it senseless to go to the store for a new piece of lumber; "You've got to have one around here somewhere," he said.

When I shut it, I'm thankful for a few seconds. It's just a door. But it represents the blessing of all the good friends I've made.

This past autumn, I installed a similar door at the ground level, just off the driveway. I called Larry. He didn't answer. I left the same message and offered breakfast, hoping he'd be around if things went south. I didn't hear from him. I struggled with the installation but got it done late in the day—I finished well after dark, to be honest.

I saw Larry the following week. He had been away up north and only got the message the following Monday.

"How'd it go, kid?"

"It doesn't open as smoothly as the one we put in together, but it works well."

"Good," was all he said.

I felt like Ralph Macchio when Pat Morita allowed him to fail at some tasks to teach him resilience and build confidence.

I didn't buy him breakfast.

The Edges

David hadn't been home for Thanksgiving in thirteen years. For only one of those years, both November and December, had he been in jail, taking his lumps for driving drunk and hitting a light pole. Most of the other years, he was intimately involved with spirits of the worst kind.

Sobriety came slowly and disappeared often. His new sponsor made good sense; Jerry, an A-lister in the royal order of Alcoholics Anonymous, told him that it would be easy to fall off the wagon when things were going well, "So don't get too cocky." He'd given reasonable excuses for skipping festive holiday dinners with his mother. Each Thanksgiving, it was something different; David had always been creative. She was gracious and didn't believe him—he knew it. Liquor made the lying easy. It could have been a song title for the Eagles. In Dave's active imagination, Joe Walsh would have sung it.

The sleet and slush pelted the car and stuck firmly to the pitted windshield; the crusty ruts created by the tires of a few previous travelers pushed and pulled the Hyundai all over the road. The worn wipers never touched the glass as they skated over a skim coating of icy crust, barely clearing it enough for him to see. The center was clear, sure. But the edges, where the wiper didn't touch, were bulking up with thick ice.

He directed the car to the side of the road, stopped, and got out to smash the buildup with the curved plastic handle of a golf umbrella that he kept in the car for the more fluid precipitation typical in the South. It worked until it shattered into pieces.

He tossed the remains to the passenger side floorboard, cupped his hands to his lips, and blew warm breath into his palms. The exercise reminded him of being chilly in his youth, but more remarkable was that he didn't smell any booze when he did it. He was nine months without a drink, and he felt good. The dog stirred in the backseat, catching on that they had stopped.

"It's not so bad driving in Maine weather when you're sober, but don't get too cocky," he said aloud to himself and his backseat companion. Prine—a genetic amalgamation of shepherd, lab, and maybe husky—lifted his head and yawned, finally sitting up to see if he was there yet. He wasn't.

The front-wheel drive of the Hyundai successfully got him back on the travel portion of the road—away from the edge—but only after spinning the summer-grade Michelins down to some bare gravel. Dave tried to keep the car in the center of the road, on the crown, as one of his drunk uncles taught him, to avoid sliding into the roadside alders. The lessons were more to avoid the cops than the alders.

Dave had been the designated driver for all the drunks in his family during his growing years, sneakily navigating slick roads that come early and stay too long in northeastern Maine. He was drinking by eleven, and his uncles and dad rewarded him for driving them around by giving him a nip or two from the bottle. They surmised that a trooper wouldn't put their kid in jail for driving drunk. As much as it seemed to make sense then, David now struggled with the consequences of their backward, backwoods logic. He'd worked through the anger. Church helped, prayers too, but a man named Chet once shared words about toast that rang louder inside his head. He had a lot of time to consider it behind bars.

"Just another hour, boy," he said, trying to reassure himself more than the dog.

Washington County was a long ride from anywhere but taking Route 2 and then Route 6 to Vanceboro accurately demonstrates the old joke, "You can't get there from here."

David considered cutting over to Route 9, called the Airline by the locals, when he passed through Bangor earlier. But that road can be dicey during lousy weather, too.

No matter how you got home to Vanceboro, Maine, it was a crapshoot. The weather in Norcross, Georgia, which Dave now considered home, only impacted steering and braking during horrendous downpours. Snow and ice in Maine forced you to be committed, in the non-institutionalized sense of the word.

Chet's Diner has been serving good chili on Route 6 since 1967, and it's the only stop for coffee, bad as it may be. Dave kept his steering inputs small and soft like his Uncle Sherman—also a drunk—had skillfully taught him. He figured Chet's was an excellent place to stop for a minute; he had plenty of gas, but his eyes stung from the strain of intently watching the road.

He'd not returned to the roadside grill in a long time and questioned whether it might be shuttered or burned down like so many things he now missed. It was also possible that Chet had long since left the chat. He'd been alive and cooking last time through, or so David recalled.

He pictured the sign over the counter, hoping it would still be there for a photo opportunity. "Chet's—home of the world's finest toast." The bread was homemade in those days. The sign made people laugh, but Chet hung it with sincerity. Dave thought of it often during his sixty-day stint in Gwinnett County Jail, working in the kitchen as a trustee, sometimes buttering toast and thinking about Chet's poignant words and his own life choices.

It was there that he began to pay attention to his shortcomings. Every piece of toast was a chance to do better. Silly? Maybe. But he'd finally applied it—like butter—in his day-to-day dealings. Years ago, Dave asked Chet directly about the sign. It was after a long night of drinking. "How can one claim they make the world's best toast?" Chet welcomed the inquiry. "Well, the bread is home-baked, but that's not the secret." "What is it then?" Dave replied, nibbling on eggs and dipping toast in the runny yokes. "Well, son, do you know how most of your standard restaurant toast has all the butter in the middle?" Chet stared into the distance as if he envisioned a large piece of bread floating before him. He continued, "It's like the butterer didn't care. You have to care, Dave, about all things."

Chet's eyes met David's, looking through him like he'd just imparted the wisdom for the ages. "I guess." Dave mustered. He'd never considered it. "Toast is toast."

The sentence scored a grimace and scowl from the Vietnam Vet standing before him.

"Dave, it matters. I butter the whole slice of toast and pay attention to the edges. The details matter, even when talking about something as simple as bread that's been browned in a toaster. I start on the edges, not in the middle, slathering the butter on all of it. Yeah, plenty in the middle, of course. But I make sure the whole slice of toast gets some attention. That's all it takes. If you're a plumber, you solder all the joints to the best of your ability. Voila!, no leaks. If you're a writer, you check your punctuation. But I make toast—the world's finest—never had a complaint."

It wasn't the Bible verses he'd committed to memory that pulled Dave away from alcohol. Sure, it helped, but it was the realization that he'd paid no attention to his own edges, or his middle, for a long time. He wanted to see the sign again and find out if Chet was still there. He wanted to tell him face to face about the little kernel of truth that meant so much.

Neon signs only shine brightly—all the letters visible—in Hollywood movies. Sometimes, the scriptwriters find a way to delete the illumination of one or two gas-filled tubes to create a humorous or off-color visual for effect. None of Chet's letters worked anymore. Instead, a poorly aimed cheap spotlight shone on the sign over the door. A lone pickup, encased in ice, was parked in the unplowed lot.

Prine jumped free of the back door and concurrently stretched and sniffed the new world. The good boy hadn't been out of the car since a Bangor fuel stop. He lapped the icy pebbles of sleet out of the air like a kid catching flittering soap bubbles. He rolled in the fresh blanket of slush, appearing unconcerned about the chill. "You've never even seen snow before, so I'm betting there's some husky in there," Dave said aloud as he stretched and huffed in the air, immediately making him cough from the burning sensation he felt in his lungs. He'd forgotten November weather can demand boots and a warm coat. He'd brought neither.

A tall fellow wearing a stained apron, leaning on the backdoor for a dooryard smoke, hollered, "Your dog is welcome to come inside. It'll get cold real quick inside that car, and he's probably not used to it. I mean, if you're planning on staying and eating something." Dave looked up, wondering how the guy knew his dog wasn't a local. "I think he's a husky, so he should be fine." "If he's from the same place where your license plates were stamped, he'll need some time to acclimate." And with that, he took another long drag before flicking his cigarette into a distant snowbank.

"Bring him in; I like dogs." He stepped back inside after stomping his black shoes on the stoop.

He yelled out again, "Remind me before you leave to give you an ice scraper," before slamming the back door shut behind him. It wasn't Chet.

The rush of hot, humid air, smelling of greasy this or that, struck Dave hard in the face when he pushed through the glass door, and the overhead cowbell clanged, announcing the only customer. Prine lifted his head and sniffed everything he could. There was already a water bowl, filled to the brim, sitting beside the stool at the end of the bar, and Prine found it.

Chet's truth still hung over the bar, but he no longer held the spatula or the butter knife. David took a photo, reviewing it as if it were to become a treasured photograph of a loved one. He then slid the phone into his back pocket.

"What'll you have, son? You've come a long way to get nowhere. And in the middle of a pretty decent storm, no less." "I have," Dave said. "I'll take an order of toast and a cup of coffee. It's been a long time coming. Maybe some scrambled eggs for the dog if it's not too much trouble."

The cook smirked, catching a bit of the Down East accent Dave had never been able to shake. "It's no trouble at all. I hear a little Maine in you." "There's a lot of Maine in me. It's my first time back in a long time; this time, I'm sober. Where's Chet?"

The man squinted and tilted his head slightly. "Good on you; me too—four years sober for me, and a friend of Bill W. You knew Chet?" The past tense reply confirmed what Dave suspected. "I did, did you?"

"My uncle. A good man. He's been gone a while. I'd love to have him back."

Dave waited for more. But the man turned toward the grill and started scraping it off with a heavy-handled spatula. Silently counting to five in his head, Dave concluded at around the four-count that the grillmaster would only be saying something else once he figured out the customer's backstory.

Dave spoke up, "Your uncle told me once or twice that I needed to pay attention to the edges, but it didn't take until I found myself responsible for making other people's toast. It's a long story. Anyway, I'm heading home to Vanceboro for Thanksgiving dinner with my mother. First time in a long time."

The man turned around, smirking. "I don't close for a while, and it looks like it's just you, me, and that dog until then. I have time for a story. Let me start some eggs. I bet you can pour us a couple cups of coffee and figure out how to work that toaster."

"I sure can."

The Last Impala

"Now, you're sure it's a '79?"

"As sure as I can be. I have the Virginia title paperwork right in front of me. Runs like a top."

Kurt had been looking for the automobile for over nine months. He didn't want to spend the money hauling the wrong car nine hundred miles north to Maine this late in the summer. "And you are one hundred percent positive it's paint code 25?"

Kurt could sense the salvage yard owner reaching the edge of frustration with the subtle increased cadence of his breathing. But, then again, maybe he was a smoker. The distinct sound of good tools on old steel arrived sharply through the phone's earpiece, causing Kurt to pull the cell phone a few inches farther from his left ear. All the pings, whacks, and thumps were accompanied by what he believed was the whirring and squealing of a brake lathe in the background. It sounded like a busy place.

Stanley Meyers stated it once again: "Yes, Kurt. It's paint code 25, Chevrolet bright blue metallic—four doors, vinyl seats, smoke-free as far as I can tell. For thirty-two hundred bucks, you won't find a better example. You say it's for your dad?"

Kurt pressed the phone against his cheek as he gazed out the kitchen window at the rusting swing set in the backyard. He recalled the days when the slide was the center of the universe for the kids. The tentacles of thin maple branches reached out from the woods, trying to recruit the crooked steel pyramid to become one with the forest.

He could get down to Virginia and back in three or four days. He'd take some vacation, maybe stop on his way home in Portsmouth, New Hampshire, to see a college buddy.

"Does the radio work well, Stan?"

Stan was losing interest in the northerner's interrogation. "Kurt, it's three grand. If the radio doesn't work, I'll find one that does. Those old Delcos are a dime a dozen. Do you want it or not? I really do need to get back to work."

"I'll take it. Do you want me to give you a credit card to hold it?"

"When are you coming to get it? That's a long ride for an old Impala."

Kurt looked at the calendar on the wall, "Well, I'm hoping to haul it home." He flipped up the page to see September. "I can be there midday next Monday. The Sox are in the cellar, but someone will be in the World Series. I'd like to get him into the car by then. Do you want a card to hold it? I can bring cash for the balance."

"He's not driving this to the World Series, right? It's a good car, but I wouldn't venture too far without a Triple-A card."

Kurt laughed. "No. No, he's definitely not driving to the World Series." Stan found it odd that any man would ask so many specifics about a plain, blue sedan. But forty-two years of buying and selling anything with wheels taught him a lot about the definitive inflection of sincerity in a stranger's voice. And there wasn't a line of buyers pounding down the front door of his shop for a nondescript, non-collectible Chevrolet.

"Just bring cash," Stan said. "And you'll have to pay the governor his share. Be here next Monday. I'll check on the radio, but most people want to swap it out nowadays for something a bit slicker than an AC Delco."

"I know, but this car is for my old man, and he can't drive anymore. But he's gotta be able to get decent reception on the AM band."

"Might it be better just to buy your father a radio? I mean, if he can't drive and all?" Stan waited for a retort in what seemed like an extraordinarily long pause. The transaction held more intrigue now. Buying a car for a non-driving family member made little sense.

"He needs this car. I won't take any more of your time. I'll rent a one-way car dolly when I get down there. Do you know if there's a place local to you?"

"Kurt, it's your lucky day. I'm the only U-Haul franchise within thirty miles. I'll reserve one for you. Got two out back right now."

The arrival in Bluemont, Virginia, came as expected. Meyers Auto Sales & Salvage was as Kurt envisioned, but cleaner. The car appeared as Stanley had described it. The bigger surprise was that Meyers was a gem of a human, a Southern gentleman. He'd put a new Interstate battery under the hood, changed the oil, and found a matching set of four used radials that looked like new. The car even had all four factory hubcaps emblazoned with proper bowties. Kurt knew Pops would appreciate prominently displayed Chevy bowties.

Meyers invited Kurt to walk over to the diner with him for a sandwich while his men loaded the Impala on the faded, orange-trimmed car hauler for the long trip home. Over bad coffee, Stan's curiosity was not to be stifled. "What's the deal with this car? I'm glad to sell it to you, but you said your father doesn't drive. This transaction makes no sense to me, and if it's something you don't want to explain, I will still buy your lunch." Stanley really wanted to hear this; he smiled as he brought the off-white buffalo coffee mug to his lips and stared Kurt in the eyes like he already had him all figured out. But he didn't. Kurt smirked; by now, he was becoming well-practiced in explaining the endeavor. He'd already had to sell the idea to his wife. That was harder than manipulating the nursing home administrator to give his non-driving father a permanent parking space in the tiny low-rent senior home parking lot.

"Stan, my father was a traveling salesman; insurance mostly, but Fuller brushes and Kirby vacuum cleaners were also prominent on his resume. He drove all over New England in the late sixties and into the early nineteen eighties. He spent his best years living out of a blue Impala. He went door to door, day to day, to keep our family in bread, milk, hamburger, and Cheerios. As far as I can recall, he wore out at least three sedans, but the fourth was a station wagon. I spent my Little League years in the way back of that one."

Stan nodded. "This does clear up why you were so specific in your brand, color, and model." With that, Stanley looked to his left past the faded blue gingham curtains of the diner. The citizenry of Bluemont bustled to and fro on the narrow Main Street. Clarity of intentions can be elusive on a long-distance phone call. Stan loved cars, but people were better. The joy in his business had always been the backstory.

"We lost my mom two and a half years ago. Now, Dad is one stroke and one minor heart attack beyond that. He's eighty-nine in March. The doctor took his driver's license last year, and we sold his car. Thankfully, he can still walk okay, but not too far or too fast. Think about what that does to a man who spent his life being mobile, listening to Red Sox games while whiling away hours and hours behind the wheel between sales appointments. He slept in it to save on motels during the lulls in sales."

Stanley silently took another sip. His thick fingers clenched the cup while he imagined himself without daily mobility or purpose. Meyers considered that the story could one day soon be his. He was knocking on the doorway to seventy. "His room is tiny, and he has a roommate who sleepwalks and watches a steady diet of QVC and any other available home shopping network program whenever he is awake. I figured I'd put this car in the parking lot so Pops could have a private spot, someplace familiar. He can listen to the Sox, smoke the occasional cigar, and maybe hang out with his buddies while sipping a cup of coffee without that lingering disinfectant smell of the nursing home. Like we are, now, you know?"

Stanley couldn't muster a verbal response, but moisture in his eyes forced him to pretend he would sneeze, and he faked one right into his napkin. In his lifetime, he had heard many ridiculous reasons why a particular person wanted a specific car. This one made good sense.

"It'll be his last Impala." With that, Kurt picked up the check, and they silently walked the quarter mile back to Meyers's shop. The car was mounted to the dolly and appropriately attached to the Ford F-150 hitch. Safety chains and the trailer wires appeared to be hooked up as well. Meyers was a full-service shop.

A tall fellow with grease stains on his forehead, probably the shop foreman, yelled, "Hey, Stan, I took the driveshaft out, wrapped it well with cardboard, and angled it into the backseat; it will tow better." "Thanks, Woody," Stan acknowledged.

Woody then looked directly at Kurt; "Make sure you reinstall it before you call me and complain that the car won't go anywhere." He waved over his shoulder before sauntering away toward the open garage bay, all the while wiping his hands on a red shop rag.

"Let's do some paperwork and get you on your way north." Stanley walked toward the office with the new owner close behind. Inside, Stan took his time in the back office, then came out with all the paperwork, passing the stack to Kurt for a couple of Commonwealth of Virginia–mandated signatures.

When Kurt pulled out the fat white bank envelope, Stanley held up his hand so quickly that Kurt stepped back. "Nope, this one's on me. That car is heading to the right spot. I've sold enough this week. Just be sure you return that car hauler to your local U-Haul depot as soon as you unload the Impala." The subsequent argument was a circuitous route to a total loss for the Mainer. Meyers was not a man who took no for an answer. "If you come through Bluemont in the next couple of years, bring me some lobster. I've heard it's better than Chesapeake Bay crabs, but I'd want to confirm that."

"Why don't you come up next summer and see where they come from?" Kurt was serious. "Maybe I'll do just that!" Stanley had never been to Maine and wasn't getting any younger.

Kurt tossed three one-hundred-dollar bills on the counter. "Buy the staff lunch."

Stan winked and nodded his head, acknowledging the gesture. "They will much appreciate it, my friend. Thanks."

The drive north was uneventful outside of the frequent stops for gas. The Ford drank fuel as if OPEC had designs to deplete the national reserves. The last stop for fuel in Clinton, Maine, was almost a hundred bucks. Kurt topped off the Impala's tank, too, with non-ethanol fuel. His father wouldn't need to be mobile, but he would need to run the engine to keep the frost off the windshield and the battery charged up.

It was October when he pulled the Chevy into the approved parking space of the Helen Weymouth Nursing Home. He backed it in so his old man and any invited occupants could watch traffic and pedestrians pass by if the game was dull or talk radio hosts blathered on too long.

The AM band came in loud and clear. But only after Kurt drilled in an aftermarket fender-mounted chrome antenna. The old wire antenna within the windshield didn't work on Amplitude Modulation worth a tinker's damn. He'd waxed the exterior to an "almost" shiny patina and finally dangled a new pine tree air freshener from the rearview. It was period correct for the days when the old man cruised the backroads of New England.

On the long, slow walk to the parking lot, Kurt's old man rambled about the Red Sox, their last-place position, and the lack of good pitching from the bullpen. He said something about Congress, too.

"Where are you taking me, Kurt? You should take me to breakfast! I wish the Dennys hadn't closed during the pandemic. The sausage here is always overcooked on Sundays, you know?"

He stopped talking when he saw the blue Chevy attempting to gleam in the long shadow of a scraggly balsam fir tree growing on the far end of the mid-parking lot traffic island.

"That looks like my old Impala, son. Those were good cars."

"Well, Pops, this is your car. But you can't drive it. Those are the doctor's orders. And if the cops in the city catch you driving around, don't call me to bail you out."

"What are you talking about, Son? You must be joking. Whose is that?"

"I'm telling you, it's yours. I'll keep it full of gas; you can come outside with your buddies, listen to the radio, drink coffee, and watch the pretty ladies walk by. But don't beep the horn and whistle, 'cause I'll take it back. I mean it, Dad. You have to promise me you will only use it as an office or a break room from being cooped up inside. And not all the time."

"Are you serious?" The old man trembled a bit more than usual.

"I'm giving you the keys. You have to promise me. No driving, just sitting and shooting the bull with the boys. Ladies, too, if you want, of course. It's got a good heater but crack a window when you are running it as we can't have you going toes-up from carbon monoxide poisoning. Also, tell Harold not to fart too much. That tends to drive the ladies away."

"Harold farts because he's lactose intolerant and drinks milk like a fat infant. It's ridiculous. I'll work on weaning him if he wants to sit in the car." He giggled with a bit of a rasp in his throat. Kurt laughed, too.

"I cleared the plan with Mr. Phillips in the front office. He has a set of keys in case you lock yourself out or pass out from Harold's condition."

By the time Kurt finished his speech, Pops had settled himself into the Impala as if it was the most comfortable seat he'd been in for a long time. He had started the engine and was lightly revving up the surprisingly smooth-running three-hundred-fifty cubic inch small block.

"She's a runner, Kurt, a real runner—thank you, son. I'll only drive it on Sundays to church." Pops looked at his boy in the side-view mirror; then he winked.

"Just make sure to ask for prayers for your time in jail, Pop. No driving. Just sitting. You have to promise me."

"Of course, son. I'm kidding. This is going to be great." The old man turned his attention to the radio knobs, looking for his favorite talk station. He'd already pulled out one of the chrome buttons and pushed it back in, locking in the preset channel like he had previous experience. It was a forgotten art.

Looking over his shoulder as he walked away, Kurt still couldn't believe that the "79IMPALA" vanity plate was available from the DMV. From a hundred feet away, he could hear the elevated, deep voices of vehement talk show hosts already booming from the speakers inside the car; that would be a problem. But not today.

Pops passed away the following spring. He'd managed to burn through three tanks of gasoline that winter but had never once left the lot. He didn't die inside the car, and for that, Kurt was thankful. He was also somewhat remorseful, for it would have been fitting.

In his final conversation with staff, Pop demanded that the dining crew stop refilling Harold's milk glass because the opening day at Fenway was the following week.

Kurt gazed out the kitchen window into a backyard devoid of the old swing set. He had trimmed back the maples, too. The Impala fit inside the grass-faded footprint almost perfectly. It needed a tune-up; the intake was definitely carboned up from idling too much. With the windows down, he could comfortably listen to the Sox games from his cedar Adirondack chair beside the fire pit.

While several members of the homeowner's association were stricken with the vapors, Kurt left their three certified letters unopened on the counter. He'd done his homework. It was only unregistered vehicles that were forbidden, and he planned an autumn trip to Virginia, maybe getting together with Stanley for lunch. He had already renewed his Triple-A membership and knew a guy who could pack a dozen two-pound lobsters so they arrived safely in Virginia.

Next Tuesday, Kurt planned to take Harold out for a coffee—no cream—of course.

A Dooryard Visit—A Down East Primer

I DIDN'T MEET TIN WHITE BY MISTAKE. WE WERE INTRO-duced, but not in an official sense. Tin happens to live in my glide path to Down East. I am lucky enough to drive by his house about fifty percent of the time I head to camp. There are other ways, of course. And I tend to mix it up.

Tina White, Tin's daughter, suggested to Tin that he read some of my posts. Subsequently, he read one or two of my books. They seemed okay to him. Then Tina asked if I might stop by sometime and surprise him. She said he enjoyed my writing, and it would be neat for him to meet me. It sounded good, but I am inherently shy. Sure, I pretend I'm not, but pulling into someone's driveway without an official introduction can be rife with dark consequences. Tina assured me he was hopeful to have a meet-up, so I kept my eye on his driveway during my comings and goings. I promised her that if I caught Tin outside, I would pull in and have a chat.

Now, I know Tin's lawn; it's groomed magnificently. I also know what he drives for a lawnmower. One summer's day last year, while driving by, I noticed Tin's John Deere parked out front. I knew he kept it undercover in the barn; this was a good sign that he was out and about. I turned around, pulled in, and knocked on the door.

Needless to say, he is a wonderful host. He invited me into the den, and we had a magnificent sit-down. I met his lovely wife, Lanie, and I stayed too long. Tin is full of good stories. Since then, I discovered that he and I share the same birth month, only one day apart! His birth name is Wilbur, but he was pinned with Tin long ago. Of course, I inquired. Tin has always been on the thin side, and that's because he never stops moving. Since he was considered as light as a tin can, the name has been his for over eighty years and probably closer to ninety. You see, Tin is ninety-five.

Tin has attended at least one of my book signings, and I think he considers us friends. I certainly do. That's why, this past Friday, I pulled in for a dooryard visit. These are a New England staple, and they tend to be quick, unplanned events when you pull into a friend's dooryard with no intention of going inside the house. They are aptly named. Tin was mowing happily away with the idea he could beat the incoming hurricane. His lawn is several acres, an example of rich, green perfection. He had just un-mired his mower from a wet spot high on the hillside but was undeterred from finishing up. I pulled up to the fence and waved him down.

As you can imagine, we had a wonderful time. I had no idea Tin rebuilt the barn in 1984. The house belonged to his dad then. The barn had become too broken down to utilize, so a teardown was the only option.

That is until Tin took a six-week vacation from work to rebuild it into the straight, true, and sturdy structure that houses his beloved John Deere to this very day.

Each time I talk to Tin, I realize that I am in no way living up to the potential that's expected of us. He is a pilot, war veteran, craftsman, wonderful husband, father, and friend. Tin is my friend. That's the only reason I felt comfortable—unannounced—pulling up into his dooryard.

And now you know what a dooryard visit is all about.

SUMMER CAME

SUMMER CAME, BUT SOMEBODY WATERED IT DOWN A BIT. I hope no one believes that I am complaining about the endless rain. The older you get, the more you appreciate it.

When the sun broke through for a few minutes on the Fourth and I felt the humidity rise, I concluded that all that rain hadn't been so bad. Within hours it returned—last night, with a vengeance.

It was a thunderstorm that made you forget the previous worst thunderstorm. We sat in the cedar chairs on the lawn for a long time, watching it strategically make its way down the lake like an electric monster, stalking us. Of course, we all counted the seconds between the lightning and the thunder, most still believing each second equaled a mile of distance between the monster and us.

When the waves started overtaking the top of the dock, we moved inside, each of us—except the youngest—fighting for a window seat. My grandfather would have called the storm a "doozie."

I care much less about perfect summer weather than I did when I was young. What I care about now is that I get that feeling—the feeling of summer. I want to revel in the joy of my granddaughter's squeals when she makes first contact with the always-cold lake water. Watch the dogs swim, holding their heads up just high enough above the water for their muzzles to snort in and out the oxygen they need to keep on paddling.

I enjoy hearing the musical sound of a distant two-stroke outboard motor when life quiets around me in the late afternoon. Unseen and unseeable because of distance or island obstructions, I picture the boat's occupants, wonder about the conversations, and sometimes consider whether they have enough gas to complete the journey without concern.

And yes, I howl and scold when I sit on a wet couch cushion, knowing that one of the dogs has used the aged furniture as a sponge to dry off their coat. I don't want perfection; I'll take my life with a side of frustration, maybe some homemade cole slaw and an A&W root beer, too.

We all appreciate the sound of a wooden screen door slamming. It's iconic and probably one of the most recognized sounds of the people from my generation. I feel sad for the kids subjected to only hydraulically softened closures of color-matched aluminum doors. Even after years of stretching and stress, rusty springs close the door more boldly, telling the world that there has been an exit or an entry, fending off all but the most bloodthirsty mosquitoes. Duct-tape patches over dog-torn screens do an excellent job of keeping the bugs at bay, at least for a few days. New holes appear overnight, and tomorrow we fight the battle again.

Being a lifelong Maine boy, I also know that Independence Day marks the beginning of a countdown to autumn and winter. I know I am not alone in this glass-half-empty mentality. I've talked about it to others who are like me. I think it's a New England thing; enjoying but planning for what will inevitably—and too soon—come next.

For today, I am alone at the camp. Family had appointments in town one hundred miles away. I was selected to stay behind and care for the three four-legged beasts, all sleeping comfortably around the tiny camp. My digressions bottled up from a week of not writing a thing leak onto the keyboard like happy tears at a joyful reunion.

Summer came. Soak it up. Wring it out. Enjoy it while it hangs out on the porch. You'll know when it's gone by when you no longer hear the slamming of the screen door.

Acting on the Adage

She was walking purposefully, and I could see her coming from about an eighth of a mile away. She appeared to be about my age, but I am basing that on the silver streaks in her short hair; it reflected the early morning sunshine enough to conclude that hers was the same color as mine, but she walked faster than I do.

I was stuck at a light, red, to be exact. From my vantage point, I could see down the street to the next light, but the walking lady was the only other human in sight. Her arms were pumping to and fro, and it was clear that the lady was walking for exercise, not pleasure.

It was only six in the morning, but spring was turning on her charm. Looking down the street, I saw flowering crabapple trees with branches reaching out just over the sidewalk. They needed a trim, but we give flowering trees a pass regarding their intrusion into our pathways. We'd be frustrated if a pine branch dragged across our head; we might even talk to the homeowner about clipping it back. Flowering trees are more acceptable intruders. It goes to show that it does matter how you present yourself.

As I accelerated, I watched the walking woman because there was nothing else to do for those few seconds. I glanced in the rearview mirror to check the load in the truck's bed, ensuring the straps held tight to the dunnage I was hauling off to camp.

Just before I passed her, she abruptly stopped as if she had forgotten something back at the house. It caught my attention. She spun around and shuffled back to the protruding pink blossoms of the crabapple tree. She reached up and pulled down a single limb, putting it next to her nose and inhaling intentionally. With that, she let go, pivoted, and got back on pace, arms pumping and legs stretching farther forward to compensate for the lost seconds.

It made me smile. My passenger had missed it, and I tried to explain that someone was taking the time to stop and smell the roses, substituting the word roses merely because I didn't want to explain it any further. He hadn't noticed any of the stopping, the spinning, or the sniffing.

I turned up the radio and sipped from my paper coffee cup. The coffee stop was the very reason I was stuck at that light, looking down the long street and witnessing a woman living the age-old adage. She almost missed it but thought better about it. Then, she made the time before finishing what she had started.

There is a lesson there for all of us. Adages become age-old for good reason.

1972 IN A BROWN PAPER BAG

BY TODAY'S STANDARDS, WHAT I BELIEVE TO BE EXCEPtional isn't at all. Comparisons tend to pale in comparison from one generation to the next. What I once felt was a stellar moment wouldn't even move the needle for today's youth. That doesn't change my level of delight when I recall a simple joy. Not even for a moment.

In this case, my brief moment of happiness was brought on by the aroma provided by a warm paper bag. I was out of town during a recent road trip. The coldly decorated hotel room brought me zero delight. The room was designed and furnished with today's more youthful traveler in mind:

- Minimal uncomfortable furniture. All items were hard-surfaced, easily cleaned, and finished in primary colors
- A frigid bare floor
- A multitude of power ports to charge devices
- A flat-screen television that took up an entire wall
- Pillows that needed the support of other pillows if there was any hope of finding a position that could hold up your head

I sent photos to my Significant One. I told her it felt like I had landed in the future, but only if the future sucked. She explained that I was in a "boutique" hotel and that she hated them too.

I went out for pizza. I needed a walk to get out of what felt like Austin Powers's modern-day shag-less palace. I found a place that felt right. The cold air around the brick pizzeria smelled of ovens venting outside what was cooking within, but I wasn't confident that the pizza would bring me the comfort I sought.

Let me be upfront with you; it wasn't the pizza that gave me the fix I needed. It was the nostalgia of the round cardboard pizza container haphazardly stapled so that one browned edge of the pie peeked out through the waxed paper liner. When the clerk handed it to me in a sturdy brown paper bag—folded tightly on the business end—my mind began to produce the memories.

The perfume of brown paper warmed by an inner core of off-white cardboard holding sauce, cheese, and crust recently cooked at seven hundred degrees gave me flashbacks to 1972.

In what I can only describe as an out-of-body experience I found myself standing beside my father at the counter of Tri-City Pizza on Broadway in Bangor. It was a Sunday night in the early winter, and we were picking up five similar-smelling pies wrapped in brown paper bags. I cannot describe the perfume that permeates from warmed brown paper, but if you know, you know.

Immediately, I was fresh out of Sunday night services, and dad had been paid, by check, as he always was on Sunday nights. Pastors' salaries are meager, probably to this day, but our family tradition was that my three sisters and I would get our own pizzas on at least one Sunday night each month.

Dad would cash his deacon-written blue paper check at the register while paying for four or five pizzas. He would take the remainder and put it in his wallet for life's expenses, but that night we were kings. I don't think my littlest sister got a pizza, as she was right around three or four years old, but the rest of us were blessed with whatever pizza we wanted.

Being eight or nine, I was plenty responsible enough to carry the stack of pizzas, two to a bag. The cold night air and slippery parking lot demanded I hold the pies close. Close to my chest and just below my chin. I used my chin to stabilize the manna, which put it awfully close to my nose. I remember that smell.

Hot mozzarella cheese and basil- and oregano-infused tomato sauce marry well within the stapled round pizza plate. For some reason, the most crucial component was that brown paper sack holding back all those odors and being heated to the point that it could add its earthy scent.

After getting into the backseat of the light blue Chevrolet Impala wagon, I carefully placed the paper-sacked stack on my lap. Now enclosed in the warm car, the brown bags were free to release the magical odor throughout the interior. If you asked my sisters today if they remember, they would.

If I recall clearly, we took the short drive to the parsonage to sit—three across—on a worn green tweed couch as we watched Sunday night variety shows. In the early years, Andy Williams; maybe Ed Sullivan. Later, I think, Donnie and Marie. Skits were silly, songs were splendid, and hot pizza warmed our innards. I think we felt loved.

That must be what I smelled as I walked back to my boutique hotel with plenty of open storage under the bed and an ugly red table that fits no home decor in modern-day America. Sure, there were plenty of charging ports, but I kept the ripped brown paper bag on the bed as I ate, trying to keep the stack of pillows advantageously angled so I could find something to watch on the enormous television. The odor of the brown bag lingered; I set it on the light-colored bedside stand as if it were a recently won trophy, but more for its magical, nostalgic, and odiferous properties.

The pizza was adequate, but the room smelled like 1972. I slept like a nine-year-old.

A Rolling Steel Box of Thankfulness

I avoid attempting to be philosophical about things. But I let too many things pass without being thankful. I was grateful for my rolling chest of tools late in the afternoon yesterday.

A peaceful moment of contentment overwhelmed me when I went to the drawer and found the exact tool I needed for the chore at hand. I also participated in a moment of solitary silence for the fellow who sold me—while under duress—that box full of tools. I'll get to that.

I've spent thirty years digging through various toolboxes in a range of sizes. I'd load them in the truck to take them to the camp in the woods and reload them for the trip home. I'd often forget the one toolbox holding the specific tool I needed at one location or another.

I frequently faced the dilemma of heading to the hardware store to purchase a duplicate tool because of my forgetfulness. It's well over one hundred miles between camp and home. It's cheaper to buy a twenty-five-dollar set of crimpers than spend fifty dollars on fuel for a round trip to find what I had left behind.

I consider myself a handyman, but only out of necessity. I've always told my friends that my doctrine is "learn by ruining." I have ruined so many things.

For those who care and those who do not, I sought a tiny chrome pick configured with the handle of a miniature screwdriver. I was under the tractor's hood—a place where I don't fit. I was preparing the rig for what looked like it might be a record snow-blowing season. I'd greased the bearings, the pivot points, the clutch, and the brake pedals. I changed the oil and hydraulic filters and checked the rear-mounted work lights.

The pressure in the enormous tires was spot-on, and there wasn't much left to do except change one headlight bulb. I'd avoided it for two years, but only because of YouTube. Men with more extensive toolboxes than mine have created how-to videos about the process. The video-makers said it could only be done by removing the entire headlamp assembly. I set out to prove them all wrong.

The short answer is that they were right. The long answer is that I spent well over an hour trying to overcome their dissuasion. I ended up removing the headlamp assembly. The late afternoon light was waning, and I returned to the house to grab a flashlight; I started the process too late in the day—I do that a lot, too. I also needed a small picking device to detach the wires from a connector under the hood. I had already tried using the tip of a pocketknife. I worked far too long with that method.

In the third drawer down of my rolling toolbox, I found a Craftsman pick and hook set. This box was originally owned by someone else. I bought it from him in an intense moment of desperation. You see, the toolbox was one of the last things he needed to sell to pay for an unexpected journey.

In short, the man came home early from another trip and found that his long-time partner had taken up with someone else. The couple had worked through most of the details by the time of the enormous garage sale, but the toolbox didn't sell. I got a call from a friend of a friend, asking if I'd be willing to drive over to buy the box full of tools. That friend accompanied me to the house. It was a bit uncomfortable, but I was assured the couple was on the same page and I wouldn't be entering the middle of a domestic dispute.

I never even looked in the toolbox. I could see that the rolling steel tool locker alone was well worth the asking price. It took three of us to load it into my truck, and I paid him a bit extra as I knew he was setting out on a journey to a new life. His ex-partner thanked me, and so did he.

The toolbox has had everything I've needed for the last five years. Last evening, it produced again. That man must have been a lot like me. I replaced the headlamp, shut the tractor's hood, and put the pick back in its proper place in the drawer.

I realized it was the week of Thanksgiving. I lose track of time in retirement. I walked back upstairs, where my wife, working from home this week, was pounding out another email to someone somewhere. I let too many things pass without being thankful. Sure, I am grateful for my pick and my rolling set of tools. Still, I am more thankful that I'm sleeping in a familiar place with a very familiar person. For today, at least, there will be no garage sale, and I'll be keeping the tools.

Recollections, Redemption, and Ricky B.

A cop needs to remain neutral in many relationships. I can admit that, over the years, I have sometimes enjoyed my time with suspects far more than my time spent with the victims of crime.

I've had numerous conversations with extremely competent police officers. Among them were some who stated an intense hatred for those who had committed heinous criminal acts. Hating the act but finding redeemable qualities in the actor allowed me to be much more successful regarding meaningful conversations that might bring the case to an acceptable conclusion for the victims.

My standard line for new investigators was to implore them to find something likable in every suspect. Some shunned my advice. Some embraced it. Those who embraced it were usually rewarded with a higher confession rate, thus bringing a higher conviction rate in court.

Police work is not rocket science. As much as crime scene investigative television programming wants you to believe that science is the end-all to solving crime, it really comes down to relationships and conversations. I stand by that.

I learned something each time I encountered a person of interest. It was essential to treat them with respect, to pay attention to where they came from. I don't mean that in a regional sense; try to understand their interests, and keep in mind their internal demons that could be uncovered during communication.

Victims want you to side with them in their disdain for those who committed crimes against them. As an investigator, you cannot afford to deplore the criminal. Deplore the act, not the actor.

I met Ricky after being assigned a simple burglary at a downtown convenience store. It just took me a while to find him.

I was new in the detective division. With that "new guy" designation, you pick up all the cases that the seasoned investigators do not want. For this case, the stolen items read like a shopping list written by someone setting up a new apartment: cleaning products, toothpaste, toilet paper, and deodorant topped the list.

The simplest explanation is most often the correct explanation. I am a simple guy. I was looking for a person with a criminal background who recently moved into new digs. Most new apartment dwellers go shopping, but a burglar doesn't. Not in the strict sense of the word. I can tell you that the suspect was good at his job. He understood the getting-ins and getting-outs of a successful "shopping" session. Remaining unnoticed is one of the signs of an accomplished burglar. Ricky was all of that. I am sure he probably hit a few places where the owners never knew he had been there; he's good.

However, when he broke into the home of a lovely couple and cleaned them out, I caught that case too. Not to minimize the importance of clearing commercial burglaries, but a home burglary involving outstanding and hard-working citizens suddenly causes your desk phone to ring; it's usually the chief. My old motto is, "The squeaky wheels get the chief."

Many have eschewed my use of maxims in simplifying my life's work, but I like them.

My partner and I did our legwork. Ricky stole the folks' car and used it to transport rugs, furniture, household appliances, jewelry, and clothing.

We discovered the car—abandoned and undamaged—over on the east side of Bangor. Not too far from where a recently released prisoner had rented a new apartment, walking distance. Probation records confirmed the rumor that we picked up while canvassing the neighborhood. This was long before Ring cameras caught every pedestrian walking down a street. So, it was old-fashioned legwork.

Confronting a suspect about a suspicion is much better when you are holding undeniable evidence. My partner, Beaulieu, and I waited until garbage pick-up day. We always laughed a bit when we picked up noxious garbage bags. We were required to wear ties, so we could only imagine what other apartment dwellers would think when they saw two guys in cheap suits driving a black Chevy Lumina removing a week's worth of Glad-bagged refuse. We grabbed all of it and stuffed it into our trunk. Some went in the backseat.

We emptied the worn-out sedan of trash and after a few minutes of stinky work, we found some cheap costume jewelry that had been reported stolen. Ricky knew the difference between good stuff and not-so-good stuff. We also found identifiers in the bag that connected it to Ricky's apartment and, thus, Ricky. We secured a search warrant based on all our information, and we set off one evening to search Rick's apartment. He answered the door, and from the get-go, I found him to be an excellent conversationalist—kind, pleasant, and extremely polite. He was a far cry from the burglars I had run into before and since.

Contrary to the belief that an immediate arrest is necessary to bring a case to closure, we did not arrest him that night. The moment you place a suspect into custody is when they stop talking about the crime(s). We had other burglaries we were working on, and we wanted to speak with him again without the shackles that immediate custody places on good communication.

I learned more about burglary from Ricky than I could have gleaned from any expensive textbook. The life of a convict on probation is tough. He wanted to change but change comes hard. Turning the page is even more complicated if you are a convicted felon with a skillset that can be employed anywhere in the world without punching a clock. It's not glamorous or the right thing to do, but it was Ricky's trade. Addictions play a considerable part in the difficulty of reform and a man's choice of occupation.

I also discovered that Ricky's past included navigating roads much rockier than my own. Our time in conversations both outside and inside the jail was enlightening. My concern for his long-term survival was vital for him to hear and feel.

Ricky helped me be a better investigator, true story. I also learned—again—that treating people the right way is complex because many people around you don't believe those "types" deserve human kindness.

Being true to your core is better, trust me. If people question you, remain true to your beliefs. It matters later on. Most detractors won't come around, so I let them sail away from my thoughts and consideration.

Ricky's sentence included nine more years in prison. He'd done other stints as well. Over the last decade and a half, I have often thought about how Ricky was doing. Cops don't go to prison to visit inmates. It would be unsafe for the inmate. He's been out almost two years now. Ricky found me again at one of my book signings. With the help of a couple of his close friends, he showed up in a downtown Bangor bookstore. It was great to see him. I know he has had a tough run, and the fact that he sought me out gave me the feeling of my own redemption in some small way. It reminded me of a Bob Seger song, only from Ricky's perspective. Seeking out a guy who put you in prison for a significant percentage of your life must be highly emotional. I still try to see things through the eyes of others.

I am sharing a note that I received from Ricky a few days post-meeting:

Tim,

I truly enjoyed seeing you after all the years that have gone by. You looked very happy and at ease in your retirement.

I have also thought of you many times over the years. It seems that from the first time I met you, I felt a deep sense of respect for you.

I also, believe it or not, respect law enforcement. You folks "Protect and Serve."

There is a certain admiration for what you all are doing to help people and maybe even a little envy on some level. (okay, maybe a little more than a little).

I respect you and the way you have always treated me. (as though there is a redeeming quality somewhere in me and others who have gone errant).

Thank you for your warm welcome. And for treating me as a friend, not an ex-con. It created a little more respect and admiration for you.

I hope that we see each other again in the future. Of course, more than just once or twice.

Much respect and sincerity,

Ricky B.

That brought me to the Bob Seger song, "Like a Rock." I wish I could write music, but Seger does it for me; he has always had better words than me. Maybe Ricky can put the words to this song in his quiver and stay on his current path. I hope so.

New Beginnings with Old Friends

It's hard to tell all the stories, but not because I have difficulty sharing them. My concern is for the other humans involved. I am but a minor player in most of my tales. There are others present, and I need to respect them when I share with you, the reader.

My book signings typically bring out the folks who read my missives regularly. But it can also be a time for old friends to visit me in my new role as a retiree.

Some of my former acquaintances and I were not always on friendly terms; we most likely met during a difficult time in their life. However, I still want to see them again someday. Often, the better terms come with passing years, introspection, and the lack of barriers such as badges, gun belts, and uniforms.

I've run into many people I dealt with in my official capacity as a cop, and contrary to popular belief, there are very few that I don't want to run into again. I did my best to treat them as kindly as possible. It paid me back in the way we could talk a bit easier if we ever met again. And we do, many times, meet again.

You can imagine that some people have a hard time changing. There are many reasons why they couldn't do so but treating them well—regardless—was always one of my goals.

When I started posting about these in-person book events on social channels, I got many notes from people saying they were coming to see me. One day, I got one that was extra special.

A woman I do not know had asked a friend to accompany her to The Briar Patch bookstore for an upcoming signing. She sent me a message as a heads-up. It seemed the man claimed that I would not remember him. Well, I did. We were on opposite ends of the law during our last encounter, but it was long ago.

After our last conversation, he went away for a stint. This sentence was longer because he'd had a few challenging tours before that one. He admitted that what he had done was wrong, but only after there was no other choice in front of him. He was a good person who had done some unfortunate things. He was no different than me in many ways, but his path had been the opposite. It happens.

His road was challenging, but he was—down deep—a decent human being. He probably would never have come to see me if I were still rooting around the police station, but in the atmosphere of a bookstore, he felt comfortable enough to come by. That's a big deal to me.

For many reasons, I am happy with my writing life. Seeing some old friends who have found new beginnings makes me even more pleased about my pathway.

ROAD SODAS

I WASN'T PLEASED TO LEAVE HER, BUT WE BOTH KNEW IT was time for me to head home. We live far, far apart; you've probably figured that out. I'm not too fond of over-explaining things, but it works for us. It doesn't work for everyone, however.

For our first thirty years, she worked here, in our town. She was very successful, but there was more out there for her; I fully understood. I had no choice but to remain in my role as a cop. You don't swap agencies when you are in your fifties. For chiefs, it's okay, but starting in a patrol officer position while tickling fifty-five is just plain dumb.

Contrary to what television programming suggests, you don't start—anywhere—as a detective. You must work your way through the ranks. It matters not that you were a detective somewhere else.

I stayed put. Maine is my home; I don't want to make another one. She is more adventurous.

Years ago, she took off for India after three phone calls from a man who needed her help teaching nursing skills to young women in the jungles and tea plantations. To say the least, these spots were a bit off the beaten track. On her first night in the old villa where they put her up, monkeys tried to steal her lipstick through an open window.

One of her fondest memories is trying to teach a class in a dirty garage bay while encircled by hard-working Indian women who wanted—so badly—to touch her blonde hair.

Still, she found a way to teach them simple techniques to make the care of their patients better and safer.

Her reward for the work was a couple of days in a hut at the edge of the Arabian Sea. She said her bathing suit wasn't suitable after realizing that Indian women swim fully clothed. We laughed. She's not been back since; she was scared the whole time. Even while overseen by colossal security guards, she was terrified. Still, she went.

I'd never been to her new apartment. It's charming. She's moved three times since she left the state a few years ago. I helped her once as there was some driving to do. One of her asks of her employer before moving into the newest role was to be able to fly home at least once a month, sometimes twice. It was a no-brainer for the company. She found a good boss who realized that she works well on the fly. Stuff gets done.

She spent some hours in the middle of a windy Maine blueberry barren during July when her phone calls were repeatedly dropping at the camp. It's hard to find a lady willing to stand on top of a granite boulder to help fix a problem from a thousand miles away. She does.

Upon my arrival at her new digs, she advised me that she had purchased a six-pack of Coca-Cola for me. She doesn't drink it. I do. I limit myself, but I love it. I brought four with me for the drive back to Maine.

She's been driving an old car for a long time. While she doesn't need a car for most of her days, it was vital for me to swap out my newer ride for her old rig. It's got some quirks, but I made it home. She's right; it makes a lot of weird noises. I turned up the radio, and it seemed to drive better.

While we all hope to be in perfect situations in perfect places, it doesn't always work out that way. You improvise, adapt, and try to overcome.

I'm not used to driving a thousand miles in a day, but I pulled it off with only one coffee. Oh, and two bottles of Coca-Cola. While I think she was happier fending off monkeys than she is with me drinking Cokes, she puts up with me. I can't ask for more than that.

Negligible Acts

I'M TRYING TO BE A GOOD STEWARD. MY PLAN WON'T change the world, and in the interest of full disclosure, I don't do it every single time, but it's a start. Frankly, sometimes, I forget.

I take my shopping carts from the parking lot corral instead of from the static display inside the store. Pushing the cart is more of a workout than sauntering unencumbered into the shopping experience. However, that's a side benefit—any health advantage is simply a product of my fertile, overfed mind. It burns maybe two extra calories.

At the wholesale club where I am a member, someone had emptied the outdoor cart enclosure and returned all the buggies to the inner sanctum before I arrived. While I walked away from the empty cart corral, not unhappy about having nothing to push, a pleasant fellow who had just finished loading his trunk called out, "I've got what you're looking for, young fellow."

He presented his cart to me, handlebar first like a maître d' might hold out a bottle of wine so you can peruse the label, "Take mine; I'm finished," he said.

"Thank you, kind sir," I said, trying to live up to the high standard he set forth in the elite manner he offered. "Hey, you look familiar to me," he said with that uptick of inflection that intimates healthy suspicion but isn't overtly accusatory. I said, "I don't know. What's your name?" He shared his, and I stated my own. "I guess you're not who I thought you were," he said.

I asked him where he was from. "Aroostook County," he added, explaining that he no longer resides there but lives in a town very close to mine. "Hmm, there are some Cottons up there, but none to whom I am related. I must have one of those faces."

He smiled, "Probably," and released the basket end of the cart, subliminally allowing me to exit the conversation.

I stuck out my hand, "It's still nice to meet you," and he agreed; I could tell by the squeeze. We both moved on after the conversational exchange. I liked him.

Today, I parked at the building supply store near the far end of the enormous lot. Sunshine accompanied me on the walk, which made it all the more pleasant. I retrieved an upright lumber cart featuring dividers to keep your boards away from your battens. They remind me of a rolling toaster constructed from the bent pipe, and they pivot on a central set of caster wheels as a bonus; it allows you to hit more things in the aisles when maneuvering four-by-eight sheets of this or that.

After loading the lumber into the bed of my truck, I walked it back to the storefront, where the conveyances were kept at the ready. The blue-vested cart gatherer was entering from stage left for the first collection of the morning, and as we crossed paths, he said, "Thank you," most likely for the return and not the purchase. In his mind, he summed up that it would be one less trip across the lot, especially since those carts must be wheeled around individually and not in the wagon train style.

I concede that neither meet-and-greet was influential in the scheme of international relations. However, these friendly exchanges were based simply on the uncomplicated task of returning your cart to the corral—or, in my case, selecting your wheeled steed from the corral at the outset and returning it later to where it all began.

The impact of almost negligible acts can be positive, even if you are doing it simply so you can ingest two or three more calories at the end of a long day of meeting new friends.

Return your carts; you will meet the nicest people.

THE PATH OF LEAST RESISTANCE

WITH ALL THE HUBBUB ABOUT THE UPCOMING ECLIPSE AND me being so close to the path of totality, you'd think I might get into my truck and invade some small Maine town with a cup of coffee in hand to catch the moon and sun in their public display of affection.

It's not happening.

I've decided to stay home and research Ellie's response to the astrological event. The dog and I can do that right from the back deck, which makes me happy. I'll watch her for telltale signs she's been impacted.

I've shoveled the pesky, well-stained behemoth of a veranda clear of snow in excess of twenty times in the last three weeks. It's time we use it for something other than debilitating my back and becoming a figment of physical fitness. I have reconnoitered my global position on an actual paper map of the happenings—I'm just one length of a black dog hair east of the Path of Totality. It simply means I'll be able to see without the use of a flashlight.

I am centered on the "Path of Least Resistance." That's what I'm calling it. It's precisely in the epicenter of where I am accustomed to dwelling on the regular.

To be upfront with all of you, I am considering driving to one of the Interstate 95 overpasses near my home. I will watch the traffic flood north toward Aroostook County. I did it when the Phish Phans migrated to Maine for "The Great Went" concert, which was far more interesting than destroying my retinas. I did note that a lot of those fans had bloodshot eyes, but it wasn't from an eclipse, I can assure you.

Seventy thousand (plus) Phish aficionados streamed right through my little town in 1997; not one of them was mad. I don't know if that's the case with Eclipse Chasers.

Even when faced with getting a summons from me for traveling well more than one hundred miles an hour in a sixty-five mile per hour zone, one particular vanload of patchouli-wearing fans still wanted to have a photo with the cop who stopped them on the way to the "Went." That was nice. It was long before selfies were a thing.

I'd like to add that I wrote that speeding ticket for going only nineteen over the speed limit so they wouldn't have to return to Maine for criminal court. College was starting soon, and I was all about helping them finish their education unencumbered by a pesky court date in the State of Maine. I seized ten cases of beer from that van because they were underage—still, they were cordial—and sober—until they got to the next convenience store.

While we have been inundated with a steady diet of televised warnings about averting our eyes from the celestial event, Ellie and I change the channel every time we see something regarding the eclipse. We are a bit sick of it. Plus, Dick Van Dyke is always playing on Tubi, and we both loved Mary Tyler Moore before she told Mainers that lobsters audibly screamed when they were thrown in a pot of boiling water. We've never heard it, but we listen to a lot of power ballads around here.

I certainly am not buying a six-pack of eclipse glasses at Walgreens—they are all out, a kind lady taking inventory told me straight to my face. She apologized—because . . . it's Maine.

As soon as the ads for eclipse eyeglasses started to appear on social media feeds, they were fact checked almost instantaneously by hundreds of responses from non-professional eyecare trolls demanding to see that these paper and plastic eye protectors were stamped and ISO 12312-2 certified. Seriously?

Heck, I can't tell the difference between a genuine Coach bag and a knock-off; how the heck can I trust the safety of my eyes to just any Amazon seller—even if they have six thousand positive reviews? I left a question: "Have these been used on a total eclipse and proven safe?" I've still not received a straight answer.

My grandfather stood me in front of a cardboard box with a mirror affixed to the interior back in 1970, but that was only a partial event. We stared through a pinhole. I was uninspired. I'll admit here that I turned around and looked directly at it at least once when Grandpa went around the corner to check on my grandmother—I've always been a rebel.

I do have some eye floaters the doctor told me not to worry about, and I attribute this disorder to that very event. The doctor says no. But what does he know? He's never mentioned ISO 12312-2 to me, not even once. I had to learn of this on Facebook. Can he even doctor without checking Facebook? I believe it to be impossible.

The lady at Walgreens told me that the volunteer fire department in her husband's town came to his schoolyard when he was a kid. The hose jockeys flooded the ground with water from a pump truck. Then, the kids were told to stare into the puddle. That's Maine for you, and we already have the potholes built; just add water.

For a while, I wanted to profit from the event. I considered printing up some mugs with my Facebook handle and screen-printing a tiny eclipse on the bottom, but then I realized I'd have to stand in a crowd of gawkers and try to collect cash. I'd rather stay home and watch the traffic stream north. I was positive that many of the mugs would have been broken on the ride up north, anyway. The roads actually suck, but like a rainbow, the treasure is at the end. You'll love the County. And the people are really, really nice.

For my friends in Houlton, Maine, "Godspeed." It seems like a good idea to invite people to your town right up until they arrive.

It's like inviting a large group of people over for supper. Everything is great until you pull the macaroni and cheese out of the oven—there's gonna be someone in the crowd who will mention that they are gluten free. I'm not ready for that kind of negativity.

Packing with Mama

I saw my Mama today. I brought my coffee. She'd already had hers.

I helped her pack up her favorite piece of leaded stained glass—a loon. It is lovely. She's been keeping it in a sunny window so the colors pop, but she was worried it might get cracked or broken in the move. She's taking it to her new home in a couple of weeks. We double-wrapped it. I made a box out of several boxes.

My mother appreciates a sharp pocketknife. She complimented me on mine when I cut and bent the cardboard to fit around the best piece she ever made. I asked for duct tape; she had some. She's forgotten that she made me a mallard and a grouse when she was in her heyday of working broken glass into beautiful pieces of art. She can't do it anymore. She stopped a long time ago.

The pleasant staff at her current abode have been accommodating, bringing her boxes for her move and chatting when they swing by. I sat in my dad's recliner and listened to them bubble with her at the door.

"The people here are so nice. I like them very much," she said, sitting back in her chair. I agreed. "I know they are." "There are a lot of nice people," she said. She's always reassured me of that. Being nice can make many people happy; I remember this when I see it manifest around me. I need reminders, and my mother does that for me.

Mama will write a note of thanks, in cursive, for the nice people; I'm relegated to using ugly, black letters on a backlit screen. My Mama and I are the same but different, and that's okay. I can't make beautiful art out of glass and hot lead; she can't make one box out of two using duct tape and a sharp knife. We all have our gifts.

"I leave that light on all night since Daddy died," she said.

"I get it, Mom; I leave a light on in my living room all the time. It's okay. I don't do it because it makes me feel safe. I do it because I like to see down the hall when I go to the bathroom late at night."

She laughed. "The light makes me feel better. You said this is a safe place, but you never know, do you?" "It is safe, Mom. In twenty-five years as a cop, I don't remember coming here for any reason. But it's okay if the light makes you feel better. I get it. Leave it on."

She's not been without my dad for well over sixty-six years until now. He was less than formidable for the last ten, but he would have put a hurt on you for the first seventy-five, I can assure you. He'd want her to leave the light on.

She gave me a photo they both loved. It won't fit in her new bedroom on an island off the coast. She wants me to have it. She's moving in with my sister and her husband. This charming picture came from when my eldest took my parents to Ireland years ago. They took the photo during a roadside stop. It's incredibly moving for me to look at, but I like cows—always have.

"Wasn't one of those cows facing away, with her butt to the fence, when you took the first shot?"

"There was one."

"I wish Robin had blown that one up. I enjoy dichotomy."

"I think they must have wanted a snack, but they came running from all directions when we walked up to the fence. It was so funny."

"I'll leave it on your wall until you head to the island if that's okay."

"It is. Of course."

I saw my Mama today. I had coffee. She'd already had hers.

TOO MANY TO SHARE

CAN YOU IMAGINE THE OVERWHELMING NUMBER OF PHOTOS that today's twenty-somethings will be able to show their kids in thirty years?

I grew up hearing Mom and Dad say, "I remember that picture; where did you find it?" I would listen to their descriptions. They recalled the event because someone else took the photo, and they were engrossed in the moment rather than being tasked to document it themselves. The photo was simply a prompt to jar their memory and the story behind the image.

Was it better? I can't answer that. Photos were singular, a simple snapshot in time, creating an opportunity for conversations and, subsequently, questions.

My son heard, "I think I have a picture of my 1970 Plymouth somewhere." I'd rummage through an old red Dexter shoe box and discover I no longer had the photo. "Well, I can tell you that my Fury had a paisley patterned vinyl roof, and we will never see that come out of Detroit again, thankfully. Here's your baby album and Mom and Dad's wedding video; I can't play it for you since we don't have a VHS player. You'll like this; this is your mom and me in Beaufort, North Carolina. Check out those shorts. We went to the beach that day. I don't recall what year that was, but you weren't here yet. I do know that."

"Dad?"

"Yes, son."

"What is paisley?"
I digress.

In 2050? "This is the sandwich I got in Paducah, Kentucky, that I told you about; this is the couple we ate with. Oh, here's a selfie I took with our server." While it may be more visually appealing and entertaining later, I miss multiple details when grabbing my phone instead of staying in the game and paying attention.

We've become more visual than conversational. Instead of a narration about an epic event, we demand photos and proof. I do it, too. The storyteller then fervently scrolls through their phone to find one of sixty-three photos of a single event. The extended pause becomes a catalyst for both of you to look through your phones to reciprocate the sharing. Soon, it turns into a duel of mutually displayed photos, with the participants searching for more pictures until the task becomes cumbersome and silly.

Is there a lesson here? Probably, but I don't have a photo. I'll dig around.

Do what's best for you, but conversations and clear descriptions can be memorable, too.

The Kinks knew this in 1968—

"People take pictures of the Summer,
Just in case someone thought they had missed it."

Second Chances

I wanted coffee, and while I don't take sugar, she was sweet.

Our exchange, while brief, smacked of a moment in time that wouldn't have come to mind for any other reason. Most often, I hear phrases that cast a negative shadow over the prospect of the morning, early rising, and the slog that can be all our lives on any day in particular. I've deduced that, often, the negativity comes from my lips.

I don't mean it, but it sneaks out. I could be trying to be funny or fit in for a minute, but I do not need to fit in. I pride myself on saying no when the group says yes—I always have. Yet, there I was. I can't tell you why I would speak negatively about the day ahead. I look forward to all of them, but like your days, they don't always turn out joyous. I've been walking through a time when I was more affected by heavy nostalgia. Time and distance do make many memories experientially more positive, and I am thankful for that.

I believe God has a way of subduing pain with time, a numbing agent that was here way before Novocain. Not only are we lucky when we get more of it, but it also comes with new experiences that have a way of diluting the less-than-pleasant days past.

My dad was a stalwart proponent of keeping a positive mental attitude—and I should be, too.

"Good morning!" Her voice was bright.

"Is it?" I sounded like Squidward. I don't know why I said that; I didn't feel that way inside. It was a sarcastic utterance that had no place in the convenience store's vestry. I watched the two words dissipate into the chewing gum rack, silently contemplating how to retrieve them from resting forever on the Wintermint Orbit.

I should have mitigated the moment; I still had the power. I could have smiled and specified that I was kidding. *How can I save this conversation?*, I thought.

She gave me the price, which was entirely reasonable for a medium. I had bills, sure, but I needed a nickel to accompany them to the cash drawer. I dug into my right pocket and found one coin. I held Thomas Jefferson between my fingers, and his five common cents saved me from adding another bill to the pile and being rewarded with more change I didn't want to carry.

"Look at that," she said as brightly as she said good morning. Her brown eyes gleamed much more than the nickel. Was she trying to tell me something?

I stood contemplating the mulligan, a chance to say the right thing. Another opportunity to save myself so early in the day had been set before me, certainly by no mortal being.

"Isn't that a wonderful way to start the day?" I said, placing the thickest of all the coins on the counter before her. I made sure it clicked against the Formica, adding a poignant sound effect to be utilized if they ever make a movie about my life. I know that thinking about post-production necessities at a time like that was silly. Oh, I also smiled.

She smiled, too. All she said was, "It really is," and I knew I'd saved my legacy, hoping it would make my dad proud.

ANCIENT VOICES

SLEEP WAS SOUND BUT SHORT.

I take a lot of heat for getting up at four. Most often, I am questioned what the point is. Today, I arose at three. Thinking something intelligent would erupt from my fingertips if I merely opened the laptop after making coffee, I gave up quickly when nothing remarkable became immediately available.

The one hour—lying awake—between two and three made me believe genius was bubbling around under my hairline, waiting to get out. I've been wrong before, and this confirmed that wrong is trending in my tiny world. I deleted a few paragraphs and increased the volume to the dump-recovered Klipsch speakers. It drove Ellie to the basement for a few minutes.

I spent over an hour last night rummaging through neatly stacked letters and correspondence between my grandmother and grandfather. The envelopes are intriguing, not because of the three-cent postage but because my grandmother kept the wonderfully written missives in stacks wrapped in decaying rubber bands, collated and indexed based on where she lived when she received them.

It made me feel slovenly in the way I manage my writing. It made me feel slovenly in the way I handled most of my life's tasks.

Diagonally penciled across the top of many envelopes from my grandfather, Leora noted that the letter was answered and the date. On the other hand, my grandfather most commonly started his letters to her with, "I'm sorry that I haven't written sooner, my love." He then briefly described why it took him two days to put the pencil on the now yellowing paper. He was a typical man, at least when it came to that.

All the letters are in terrific shape, and the box is only a fraction of what is stowed within a steamer trunk in my attic. Then there are the crumbling scrapbooks of photos.

I've written about the hollow and empty apartment at the end of my house. My parents lived there for a long time before moving to a more easily managed place. I've taken over a back bedroom in there for a writing room.

When the Significant One is home, managing meetings via computer in the dining room, I find writing difficult. There are too many voices using terminology that I shed like a wool coat in spring when I left behind any need for listening to others use terms like "not in my wheelhouse" and "couched." Who came up with that one? My idea of couched includes the word napping. I digress.

The tiny bedroom was only for storage, and the box of letters was in the closet. Once I moved in an old recliner, table, and lamp, I set out to neaten things up. I found the box and dragged it out beside my chair to go through when words weren't coming out and entering the MacBook adequately.

So, I've traded modern voices that annoy me for ancient voices that molded me. It's an excellent way to learn more about yourself. And that is directly in my wheelhouse. I'm now returning to the couch.

PIE

Now, it's just me and the pie.

It didn't start that way, of course. It came as a gift from the Significant One.

I mentioned apple pie, sure. I've never made one, and I'm not starting now. A man needs to know his limitations.

When she showed some passing interest in the idea, I put on a little more pressure. Then, she showed up with a bag of apples. My low-key campaign had a winner—me.

Then, I pushed the envelope. I can be too much. I am a small-dose kind of guy. I'm fun, but I've seen people's faces when they feel I have an agenda or when I plan to stick around long beyond the original plan. I felt myself recoil—slightly—when I said it. "Could we have crust from scratch?" I winced, looking away, knowing I might have crossed the line. I felt dirty for asking. She was only in town for thirty-six more hours. She had other things to do, too.

As I squinted, slightly blinking my eyes like an old dog who knows he shouldn't have been on the furniture when the folks walked in unannounced, I heard her say, "I'll make a good crust for you." The following words then slipped through my lips, "Like your mother's?" I felt like I'd said George Carlin's seven dirty words that you can't say on television. Don't bother to look them up. Things have changed, and everyone uses them on television now.

I waited for her answer for what seemed like a lifetime. Instead of feeling the impact of a rolled-up newspaper, I watched her going through the cupboard, searching for the essential ingredients.

"That would be good, wouldn't it?"

I felt the weight of the world lift from my shoulders. Sometimes you say the right thing the wrong way or the wrong thing the right way; this was the latter. "Maybe we can have Sammy over; he likes pie." I was getting cocky.

But she said, "We should; we certainly can't eat a whole pie by ourselves."

When you have pie, you shouldn't eat it alone. Two people? Yes, but you need more. Add a third, and you have a reasonable crowd for pie. Herein lies my dilemma. The pie is fantastic. Sammy came for dinner. We had pie. The Significant One pulled her famous disappearing trick the following day, leaving on a jet plane.

That leaves me and the pie—alone. She placed it in the 1970s-inspired Tupperware pie vault. It gives me good feelings of pie days gone by.

My mom had a Tupperware pie container. Mom had Tupperware for every single food group. I don't think we ever had the single-slice Tupperware traveling pie containers, but I've seen them. There were enough of us in the house so that no single slice of pie was ever left behind, let alone enough left to take to school like the smug kids with the single-serving pie containers from Tupperware; they had small families.

No, I am not having company over for more pie, and I shouldn't be eating the pie for breakfast. Again.

Pie every day is a beautiful thing, but it's not a good idea. However, I cannot let good pie go to waste, especially with a homemade crust like her mother's. Instead, I am slowly eating the pie directly from the glass pie plate—two to four bites at a time. Don't judge me; I try to eat it properly in a symmetrical fashion by taking diagonal cuts with my fork. It doesn't matter; no one else is coming by for pie. Oh, I could have gone in hard and just taken bites from the middle, but I'm a guy who thinks pie should come out of the plate in wedges, even when I am doing it with a fork sans knife.

So that's my story. I'm now five and a half days into the pie. I'll get through it. I've skipped lunch for pie twice, and I sneak intermittent bites late at night before I take out the dog. I'll admit I've had an extra bite or three when I bring her back inside after going out. That's why I leave the fork on the edge of the sink for a few minutes before placing it in the basin to wait for a wash.

For now, it's just me and the pie.

It'll be gone by Saturday.

Cleaning Windows

With Lewiston, Maine, on the hearts and minds of a whole nation, we've experienced some heartfelt celebrity outreach.

Pro footballers from the New England Patriots gave shout-outs of support to the Lewiston Blue Devils and City of Auburn Red Eddies high school football teams. It all took place before the cross-river rivals took the field, trying to get back to the business of life after the tragedy of a horrific mass shooting. Heck, Will Ferrell even piped into the conversation.

For a city and its people, it's reassuring to be noticed by kind and talented people.

James Taylor showed up with his guitar to sing the national anthem. That's a magical thing. Delivering a small dose of happiness to an entire city cannot be discounted in such horrific times.

Prominent names with big personalities have gone to war zones, raised money for important causes, and provided the service of giving people smiles when they need them the most. We need them, and we appreciate their support.

It's not what I write about, though. As a tiny speck on this globe, I am elated to highlight the little things.

My kid is a Maine State Police detective, and in his role, he was sent, like so many cops, to respond to Lewiston amid the tragedy and subsequent search for the murderer of eighteen loved Mainers.

Cops from all over Maine showed up. It's what first responders do.

Maine is vast, and the jokes about lone travelers getting the advice that "you can't get there from here" when receiving directions from a stoic Mainer are steeped in truth.

My son had a long drive from Maine's Canadian border to get to the spot where he needed to be. At the start of his shift that night, he had no idea that he'd be heading southbound for two hundred fifty miles, and of course, he had to stop once for fuel at a convenience store. He found one just off an Interstate off-ramp.

During a quick pit stop in one of Maine's well-policed small towns, he ran into another young cop working his own night shift. By then, that officer certainly knew what was going on in Lewiston. Still, Maine can't send every police officer to one city, even though the incredible and overwhelming response probably looked like that to outsiders.

So, in their brief meeting, the municipal police officer took an opportunity to do something for someone else; he offered to grab my son something to drink as he hurriedly filled up his cruiser to continue his journey. It was an offering of a boost in morale. Although not musical, celebrity-related, or sports-centric, it was equally appreciated.

My son declined, but not before thanking the officer for his thoughtful offering. He had grabbed some drinks for the trip while he packed his bag for what was going to be at least an overnight or three.

At that point, the city cop, determined to be of some assistance, did what any good Mainer would do. That is, he did something. The young police officer—sequestered in his town from traveling to Lewiston for good reason—said,

"Let me wash your windows." And with that, he did, both front and back, of course. He even sought to eliminate glass hazing by reviewing his work and polishing any remaining squeegee smears with a clean paper towel. Any cop worth his salt knows you must be looking forward and backward with some regularity, and sparkling windows are a must.

He went the extra mile so others could go further. I bet he does this in his day-to-day as well.

With very few other words outside of "thank you," my son hit the road for the last eighty miles of his journey. I know it had a positive impact on him. He could see with clarity because of that small moment of cop camaraderie and concern.

People shine when the chips are down, and I am sure there were many other examples just like that all over our great state. To be clear, we all know that if that cop could have headed south to serve the mission in Lewiston, he would have without qualm or complaint.

On my son's return trip home, he swung by my house. We talked briefly about the things he'd seen and done in Lewiston, but what came to his mind was his story about a thoughtful cop he'd never met before; he'll be sure to speak to him again under better circumstances.

Knowing it was the story I wanted to hear, he shared it with me. I've listened to stories like the others too many times. I'm more of a "let's see the stories that fell into the slot between the driver's seat and the transmission hump" sort of guy. So, while celebrities and sports stars make a positive and needed impact on the people who need it the most, there are other stories. Those little tales from that night and the following days don't have a publicist, but maybe they should.

It's just a story about a cop who needed to remain in his town—policing a community eighty miles north of a horrific scene. He wanted to do his part. And he did. It's admirable and noteworthy. No one will sing about that.

It brought to mind lyrics from a favorite Van Morrison song:

"What's my line?
I'm happy cleaning windows
Take my time . . .
. . . I'm a working man in my prime
Cleaning windows."

The Concierge

I suspected the lady came out of retirement to take a job that most wouldn't. I couldn't do it, and the fact that she became a comforter in an emergency waiting room for the sick, wounded, and those in crisis—and their supporters—is enough to reassure me that she was the right one for the job.

I wondered to myself how they found her. I know the difficulty in finding employees these days. But to find a perfect fit? That answer is elusive. Her lapel pin only read "Concierge." I was there merely as a supporter of someone special to me. I was acting as a personal concierge, driver, and advocate. While several have labeled me a man without empathy, that's not entirely true. I'll admit that I keep it well hidden, but not purposefully.

You see, I'm not a comforter—thirty-four years in public service wrung most of that out of me. Proper empathy comes from the heart, and mine morphed into more of a mechanical conveyance of assistance when someone needed it. I'm elated when someone else gives the hugs; I'd much rather push back the crowd to make sure the infirm get to where they need to go for help. That's what I was doing that day.

I watched the concierge while the medical staff cared for my charge. I focus much of my attention on the people around me. I like to observe the nuances that come with the ebb and flow of life. It's rooted in my genetic code of being a daydreamer.

Sure, the large flat screen in the center of the room was tuned to some morning talk show—the one where the husband and wife took over after Regis and that handsome host moved on. I don't even know the couple's names, but no celebrity guest star could hold a candle to the importance of the lady handing out warm blankets and kind words to those waiting for service.

She smiled and tilted her head at the perfect angle to convey she was listening. There's an art and science to that move. In our limited time in one another's presence, I envied her grasp of being genuinely empathetic. Some were coughing enough to make even a vehement anti-masker ask for a face covering. There were a few who were vomiting into blue plastic bags. Some slept, some groaned, and some supported family or friends who needed care. Meanwhile, the lady gave a free master class in the craft.

The concierge maintained a brilliant level of customer service, exuding empathy from her core. Her upbeat manner captivated me, even while she faced a myriad of society's ills. Across from me, a young couple, sitting on each other's laps under blankets, were snapping each other's face masks in a strange, flirtatious two-act play. Oh, to be young again while waiting for emergency care. I watched them, remaining confused about the reason for the strange ritual.

Their giggling camouflaged whatever the emergency was, but it was none of my business; they were getting through it together, doing their best. One of the two must have been sick, but I couldn't tell which one. The male came in with muddy boots, and while he sat there, the mud dried and began to fall off and crumble all over the reasonably clean floor. I watched the mess grow around his feet. While it wasn't intentional, it was a substantial amount of grit and pebbles.

Once they received service and left, the concierge emerged from some cubby and surveyed the newly created miniature gravel pit. I knew it wasn't her job, and I heard her call for someone from housekeeping. Not surprisingly, no one showed up. I am sure they were dealing with more significant things, too. This isn't about what didn't happen; it's an essay about what did.

She made eye contact with me, and we made small talk about the mess, but she didn't complain about the dirt, the man who left it, or the fact that no one would be coming to mop it up. "I'll grab some wet towels to clean this up myself. There are better ways to do it, but housekeeping must be busy." She looked right at me with a twinkle in her eye. She was pleasantly mischievous, taking in all negativity around her with pleasant aplomb.

I'd have relished having her as an aunt or maybe even a fun-loving cousin. I'd sit at the kid's table with her. She would make me laugh. I remain amused by how much you can learn from short interludes with the right people.

I said none of that; I just shook my head and smiled. I waited for the negativity, but that was merely a projection of my feelings of how I would have been acting by now. By the way, her negativity never surfaced.

A short time later, she returned with damp towels and quickly wiped up the mess. Before she got up from her knees, she looked at me and said, "You know, the saying is true. After seventy, never sit down or get down on your knees without a plan to get back up." And that's where my mechanical empathy should have quickly kicked in. As I contemplated helping her up, she grabbed the arms of nearby chairs and swiftly returned to her feet, rolling the towels into a ball. I barely got "Nice work" out of my mouth before she was off to an unseen backroom.

She brought my charge a blanket from the warmer, tucking it around her chin and pulling it down enough to cover her legs. "Let me go get you another one," she said. Off she went, showing up shortly after that with two more blankets.

"So nice and warm," she said as she gently tucked in loose ends to provide complete coverage. Then, she stood back to take a more global view, ensuring she didn't miss an area that needed warmth. She smiled to indicate that her job here was done—for now. My charge thanked her.

Once she hustled off to the next patient, I looked at my mom and said, "They really found the right lady for this job, didn't they?" She agreed with a nod, her eyes barely open, making up for the rest she'd missed the night before.

"I think she's French," I said. "I can hear a bit of an Acadian accent." My mother agreed. She grew up in a robust French-influenced area of Maine, as I did for a time. "She's like everyone's favorite Mémère," I mumbled as I watched her treat each patient in precisely the same way. We were treated no better than anyone else, but that's because, to the concierge—everyone here was special.

And that, my friend, is today's lesson in empathy. I'm going to try to do better. Mémère would expect no less.

You Can Get There from Here

My early morning run to Portland was a welcome change from heading east. But I won't make a habit of it. It cost me sixteen bucks to park.

Thankful is the man who parks for free; I have had a lifetime of that, so I am not being a whiner. I detest giving my money away to someone much more intelligent than I am regarding land acquisition; props to them. It's part of city life. It's just that I am not integrated into that lifestyle.

My appreciation for my ho-hum existence overwhelms me from time to time. It started in Newport, Maine, when I wanted a coffee. Pulling into the slightly slumbering city on Sebasticook Lake, I changed my mind. I turned around at the Irving gas station to get right back into the southbound lane of I-95.

The line for Dunkin coffee was backed up to Corinna; at least, it looked that way through my windshield. I wanted to use the facilities and grab a cuppa. I decided to swing into Topsham, seventy-one miles further to the south. I have an iron bladder; it comes from years of having other people control my time. It's a mindset. The exit in that fair city looked clogged from the commuter traffic backed up on the overpass. It's their city, and I let them have it. I continued toward the Brunswick, Maine, exit. I knew of a fast-food joint where I could grab a hot cup before my podcast appointment at nine.

I pulled into America's favorite arches, exited the car, and found the restroom clean and pleasant. With clean hands and an insatiable desire for caffeine (my second cup of the day), I walked to the front counter to find no humans. No humans besides the two waiting at the kiosk trying to input their order into the bright screens of the immobile lobby robots that have taken over for personal interaction with employees with an M on their chest. The paper hats have been gone for a long time. I still have an indentation on my forehead from the proud way I wore mine. I digress.

The generic Gen Xer was having difficulty putting in his order. The Millenial behind him had reverted to using his phone's app to make his order. Clever, those Millenials.

This Baby Boomer kept looking toward the counter to see if humans might arrive from the future or past to take my order—no such luck. I was on a tight schedule, so I left. I get frustrated with the technologies that take much more time than a human, even an inept and shy human-in-training, would.

It's my beef; you don't need to climb on the train with the Luddite, but I know I am correct. Sit next to me; we can run our mouths about how technology has worsened our lives. We can shout at each other and then go home and listen to eight tracks of Elvis or maybe Buck Owens. I think I have Earth, Wind & Fire's "Volume 1" in a cardboard box, some-where. Let me take a look-see.

I got to my appointment, did what I am known to do (talk way too much), and then hit the road with over an hour left on the meter. In my younger, more stubborn phase, I would have stayed if only to get my money's worth.

I skipped the Interstate on the way home. I got off in Gardiner and headed right to the A1 Diner. I needed a shot of nostalgia. Despite all the things missing from my America, the aluminum pod of gravy and fries did not disappoint. Yes, I had meatloaf, mashed potato, and fresh spring greens. I was at a diner. I can get clams anywhere. I parked for free under the bridge.

When I went to the bathroom, one of the kitchen staff opened and held the door for me. He smiled and continued to drag on a well-deserved Marlboro. You see, to use the john at the A1, you must go outside to go back inside to get to the lavatory. I like that. There is no need for costly updates; "Deal with it, Chummy."

That cook was outside, trying to cool off. It was an atrociously hot day in Maine. And air conditioning was not in the cards. The thoughtful management closed the diner down because of that heat. I was the last one served, and no one tried to rush me. I read an actual newspaper and cleaned up my plate real, real good. I tried to be a considerate patron by skipping dessert, as I knew the staff wanted to get out of there, but they didn't let on. This mope was allowed to enjoy his meal. I paid cash.

With my faith in my fellow man renewed, I drove back to Bangor on back roads. I passed Bolley's Famous Franks and turned around in a used car lot just beyond. I recalled having some of their grand raspberry puff pastries with my wiener meals of the past. They had seven in the display case; I bought three.

A pretty lady, clearly dealing with the kitchen's heat, asked me if I wanted the rest of them.

"Look at me; I could eat all of them, but not today." She smiled, and so did the chef. He looked more impacted by the heat. But he smiled, nonetheless. "Is it hot enough for you? I don't envy you today," I said with a smile. He smirked again.

He had the shaved head and the face of a guy who would be fun to be around while watching a football game. I could tell he had some jokes and quips I would appreciate hearing.

The hot dogs at Bolley's are fried in peanut oil. It's a place I frequented a lot in my days as a cop. We often had to go to Augusta for autopsies, and we enjoyed hot dogs and French fries afterward. Don't judge. The iron bladders were custom ordered with iron stomachs and a short memory of what we had just stared at for an hour. I hit the road via Route 201 and passed beautiful China Lake and the farms and homes that sprinkle the vast countryside of central Maine. The road has recently been paved, so the ride was terrific.

I pulled back into my driveway to find Ellie basking in the winds of the air conditioner. I put my pastries in the fridge and snoozed for a while. I took two pastries to my mom and dad in the late afternoon. They now live in a friendly community, holed up in a pleasant place in Bangor; I knew they would be open to taking some of the calories off my hands.

After a visit and no promises of how the raspberry puffs had traveled or kept, I motored home to dig around the Fridigaire for leftovers that would fulfill my desires. Finding none, I did the only thing I could do, went out to get some Chinese cuisine. The shy young fellow at the register even knew how to make change.

Sometimes, you can get there from here. Don't let anyone tell you anything different.

I appreciate all the cooks and servers who make my life easier. Thanks!

Vast, Dense, Lush

There are many summer days when I must drive away from the woods of Washington County to attend to business a few steps back from the Jagged Edge.

While my everyday life is in central Maine, my heart is on the coast. I cannot live there full-time for a myriad of reasons. But on summer nights, when I sit by a smoky fire and stare across the lake, I feel like I should never have to go home.

Before you start yelling at me to live my dream, know that some goals are not attainable. And even if they were, I have responsibilities that I cannot shirk. I've accepted it, but smoldering hemlock and beech mixed with cool easterly breezes fuel the dreams of many; I am but one. Reality can bite.

I had to return to Bangor for an appointment this past week. It was on the sunniest, most perfect day of the week. It was a top ten days of the year kind of day.

My Significant One headed out in her kayak, and I jumped in the truck for the one-hundred-mile trek back home. Ellie stayed behind and didn't seem bothered by my tailgate heading up the dusty hill as I made my way toward the fresh macadam of a feeder road to Route Number Nine— The Airline.

Late in the day, my chores in urban Maine were complete. I filled up on discount gas, choked at the price, grabbed a coffee, and got back on Number Nine a little past 6:00 p.m. Eastbound travelers were few, and I found the alone time that I craved. Much of my writing takes place on the road.

Not the physical act of putting words on clean white screens, but many sentences are created between songs, sips of coffee, and views that city commuters would envy.

I decided to play a lonely word game. With no one else on board the Timmy bus, I began using single words to describe what I saw. Yes, I said them out loud when I wasn't singing along with Sirius/XM's Classic Rewind. After twenty minutes of travel, I started paring down the list.

Long about the Airline Snack Bar, I finalized the list before my right turn toward Deblois and the Metropolis of Cherryfield (the self-proclaimed Blueberry Capital of the World; yes, ironic).

Vast, Dense, Lush. I laughed to myself (not hearing my snicker over the volume afforded to Tom Petty) that the list of words could be names for three exotic dancers at a northern Maine dance club—I've never been inside, but the descriptions of some of the dancers have reached many in the outside world.

On the peak of the hills is where I settled on *vast.* I looked out for miles, seeing nothing but forest canopy.

I picked *dense* in the low valleys while peering down into the green growth that ever creeps toward the edges of the road. You can't see more than three feet into the woods in most locales; that density keeps much of Maine a secret. Mainers like secrets.

Lush came from the deep green colorization we've experienced this year from endless record rains.

I was happy with my shortlist, and from then on, I focused my attention on the sides of the secondary roads, looking for the creatures that cross without warning. It's been a big year for whitetails, but moose are more of a concern. If you wonder why so many Mainers drive big pickup trucks, wonder no more. We love the environment, yes. We also want to live through a crash with Bullwinkle. We also carry heavy things, so there is a myriad of reasons why you see so many pickup trucks while romping around the pine tree state.

My hour and forty-five-minute flight passed like it never happened. Soon, I was stirring up the dust of the camp road, briefly running into a group of vibrant teens in a side-by-side utility vehicle who were ripping and tearing on the dirt road. Our pleasant chat waylaid my return to the cabin.

They were polite and friendly. We all agreed that those who buy the gravel should have some say in whether it is spun into the woods. My vote was for it to end. Surprisingly, they agreed. Sometimes, a person's approach can arm the mouths of teens, but we remain friends.

As I pitched down the hill, just past the steel gate, the dense, lush raspberry bushes pinstriped the panels of the dusty truck. There will not be a vast amount of berries this year. Plenty of rain gave them hope, but the berries we have picked so far cannot be described by the words on my finalized list.

The drive is a chore on some days, but on this day, it recharged me. I slumped on the old couch in front of the sliding doors to the porch and perused the last twenty pages of a beat-up paperback that's been in my pocket for far too long. I fell asleep under a light blanket that I used to cover my toes when the sun dropped out of sight. My slumber was no different from my ride; vast, dense, and lush.

Here's to long rides, good tunes, and lonely word games. Rest in peace, Tom Petty.

Leora's Words, Not Mine

I HAVE NEVER USED THE TERM IN MY ENTIRE LIFE. BACK IN the days when I did wear pajamas, I called them just that— pajamas. This might make sense to you soon, but surely not before I can explain myself.

The sentence—stated directly to the dog as she ran up the steps after taking care of some business—came from somewhere deep in the recesses of my mind. It was a statement that I'd not heard since at least 1973.

I'd slipped into a dream state while leaning over the porch rail and surmised I'd spent the day doing nothing important. Subliminally, I self-certified myself as lazy. I took a short drive to pick up a trailer and mowed the lawn, but nothing earth shattering. I didn't even soil a kitchen knife when I squeezed creamy horseradish sauce across one slice of the whole-grain oatmeal bread utilized for my roast beef sandwich; too lazy. It was intentional to avoid doing dishes.

These were the things I was thinking of as Ellie investigated her domain. I couldn't see her, but I could hear her rustling in the dry leaves within the brushy border of my property. It also dawned on me that I should stand in amazement that there could be any dry leaves or duff anywhere within the boundaries of Maine. It's rained for weeks—and that's not hyperbole.

I experience those moments of catatonic thought. I stare at nothing in particular and listen to the sound of crunchy leaves and a light breeze fluttering the maple leaves. This year, they've been made enormous by so much liquid nourishment, so I think they flap louder. Passing traffic rattled me back to reality. It's silly to write about, but it's clear to most of you who read my stuff that I write about many foolish things.

I've found myself alone, much more than I've been accustomed to for the past year. Not for the last few days, though. Since last Thursday, I've been surrounded with family.

That party broke up late yesterday afternoon when my son and his family headed north for home. And closing ceremonies were finalized when I put my Significant One on an airplane at 5:00 a.m. this morning. We'd had a good time.

I found myself just standing there, bummed out a bit. That's not like me, but I am human. Some of my reflections were focused on the past year, being retired, and some about being alone. I like it mostly, but it can land you in a place of gloom if you don't stay busy. I decided that tomorrow I would write for a while, then head to camp to put an underground electrical wire across to the bunkhouse. For that to happen, I need to rent a piece of ditching equipment for the one-hundred-twenty-foot run. That'll get me back in my stride. That will keep me busy, and I need to be.

As I waited for the dog to come back up the long set of stairs, I came to grips with the fact that the rest of the evening wasn't going to be productive. Why force it? I would change into some writing clothes and take it easy—even easier than I already had it—it was lounge pants and hoodie time.

What came out of my mouth, looking at the dog, and surprising even me, was, "I think I'll change into my night clothes."

I took a minute as I walked back inside the house for the meaning of that sentence to wash over me. My grandmother,

Leora, used that term exclusively when there came inevitable discussions about changing for the evening. When it was time for bed, she'd say, "Timothy-Titus, it's time to get into your night clothes." I knew she meant pajamas. She said the same thing to all her grandkids, so I had prequels of clarity regarding the terminology. Sometimes she said, "Bedclothes." I never once heard her say pajamas.

"Night clothes" was the perfect moniker for what I wanted to put on and a phrase that must have lingered in my mind for a long time. It's never manifested itself into words coming from my lips, I assure you. It stopped me in my tracks, but not because Ellie cared what I was about to do.

My grandmother passed away in the mid-80s, both hers and the decade. She used all kinds of antiquated terms, just like your grandmother did. A slip of the tongue set me thinking about Leora and all her nicknames for me. One was a "Skinnymalink." The other was "Timothy-Titus."

Her voice ran through my head for a while, or at least for a few minutes, when I tried to recall it. I don't know if I got the voice right, but I could hear what she said. That's what matters. It set my mind to wander further from the center for a few minutes. It wasn't a resounding message from beyond; we're talking about night clothes here. Pajamas. Sleepwear. But it was a message from within that I heard loud and clear. I suspect Leora doesn't want me moping around feeling sorry for myself; she never sat still, not for a minute. However, I believe that she wanted it known that it was okay to give up on the day. Be comfortable. Prepare for tomorrow.

This Skinnymalink will get at it bright and early in the morning, earlier than most humans do. For now, it's okay to get into my night clothes. Timothy-Titus likes to be comfortable, and Nana said that it was okay.

Fully Chained Melody

It stands to reason that I was ignoring the sounds. Sometimes, I have the house music turned up too loud, so I am sure I've missed many of the joyous exclamations blurted out with nary a worry about how it sounds or whom it bothers.

My often open bedroom window is within earshot of not one but two swing sets. Old school fun, facilitated by a rusting steel pipe tripod, strung with medium-duty chain, and topped off with a sling seat made of heavy-duty rubber. The archaic entertainment device pre-dates most all types of kid-centric fun.

Swings have been a staple for a long time, most likely starting with merely a rope strung from a tree limb— hopefully over a creek or a pond—for secondary entertainment value. I suppose sturdy vines were used before, but this isn't a history lesson.

Since my granddaughter has been milling about, the accessible local swing sets are getting a workout. The self-described "excellent swinger" has dragged me to the contraptions if only for my skill at pushing her to higher heights than she can propel herself.

I'll take that job.

One swing set belongs to the best neighbors ever. Regular occupancy of the swing set is limited as their grandkids live some distance away. The lilliputian-sized climbing wall is there when the little lady takes a quick break from soaring.

We have been given full-access permission, which makes us all happy.

The other swing set is some distance away, but my window is still within earshot of any pilots who take the seats. In the last couple of months, I have had a chance for occasional naps. Sometimes the half-hour snoozes occur during a swing session for some unknown child or adult. I have listened to the sounds, sometimes in a state of complete relaxation, and I have surmised that swinging never makes anyone feel worse. I don't see their faces, and the distance and grove of trees between us must muffle some of their excited utterances. Still, from what I hear, I am labeling almost all of it as pure joy.

One night a few years ago, I heard an argument between a man and a woman. They were using the swings as a meeting place. I couldn't make out the words, but they echoed angrily. The thing is, that never happens when the swings are being used for their specific purpose. I never hear an argument when the chains are rhythmically squeaking. You can't be mad when you are swinging.

My thought, probably right after a nap that created a groggy yet creative writer, was to install swing sets in the lobbies of offices belonging to therapists, counselors, and lawyers. Especially lawyers.

I listened to my granddaughter singing her thoughts while swinging as high as she could. She couldn't control herself. At one point, calling out the name of one of her best friends as being unable to swing as high as she was at that very moment. It wasn't malicious, not even a little. Her best friend wasn't even there to see her altitude or hear her off-key exhalations. She was so happy to have someone pushing her farther in the air than she could swing by herself.

Every now and then, I capture her on the backswing, stopping her cold. Then I pull her back higher than before and let her go. The screams of joy could heal the sick and make the blind see. That's what swings can do.

If you have a moment in the coming weeks and are looking for a place to eat a sandwich or read a book, drop by a park rife with kids on a swing set. Park your car some distance away, roll down your window, and bask in the sounds of happiness released into the ether. It will change your day.

The First Dip

The dip wasn't planned, like most things I do. On the drive to the camp in the woods, I determined that if I did put the water line into the lake, it might be the earliest date that I've ever done it. For crying out loud, it's still April.

I knew the ice went out around the fifteenth of the month, and I usually wait until three weeks after the ice goes out to take my chances on priming the pump and charging the water system. Ice can still form in the pump that sits outside. Ice and impellers don't mix. Ask me how I know.

The thing is, I like showers. The hotter, the better. I need running water to take my showers, and much work is planned over the next month or so. The issue goes back to my infancy. No, really. It does. In my early years, I was found to be a sweaty little baby. That's not name-calling. Well, it is. My mother called me a sweaty little baby. She even took me to the doctor to inquire why I sweated so much. I don't recall any of this; the doctor told her, between puffs on a Winston, that some babies just sweat more than others. That was the last medical attention that I received for my lifelong condition. Well, that and showers.

I don't mind working hard, but I want a shower at the end of the day. In the early years at the camp, there was no running water, so there were no hot showers. The summer that I cedar-shingled the place, I merely dove in the lake at the end of the day.

Ivory soap floats, and I did too. It was in the heat of the summer, so it made sense. I'd do the same thing in the spring and fall after a day of hard labor. The cold didn't bother me as much on those days.

Now, I demand a hot shower. Call me a diva. I scanned the outside temperature gauge on the truck. It read forty-nine degrees when I pulled into the camp yard. I got to work on the chores that could be done without excessive sweating, and then I determined that the next time I came, it would be nice to shower when I got done. That led me to prime the water line and the pump and place the black, one-and-a-quarter-inch water line into the lake.

I usually connect the foot valve to an old iron anchor this early in the season and toss it out a few feet into about three feet of water—the whole plan went awry when the heavy-duty zip ties broke away from the water line mid-toss. The anchor went deep and the foot valve went shallow.

Retrieval was necessary. The plan was set. I was going into the lake, probably up to my neck. I returned to the cabin and dug around for some swimming trunks. Wet jeans would chafe me for the entire one-hundred-ten-mile drive home. Chafing is problematic.

I found the old dark blue trunks covered in tiny white and red smiling whales. The irony was afoot as I slipped into the suit. I say slipped, but I mean squeezed.

From there, it was just inner fortitude that drove the whole process forward. I can tell you that the water temperature was well below optimal, and you could determine that because of the pain that overwhelmed my bones. Ellie watched in silence as she lay in a sunbeam. She'd been in the water already. I couldn't ask her for pity.

I sat on a rock in the sun for a few minutes post exit. It's hard to believe that forty-nine-degree air and a stiff wind could feel so tropical. I changed back into appropriate camp wear and started attaching faucets, shower valves, and the outside hose. I almost took a hot shower before heading back to town. I didn't.

Hot water is cleansing, but cold water is refreshing; it reminded me of the days when it wasn't so easy grabbing a hot shower, and I embraced the thought of it as Ellie slept in the back and I sipped a hot black coffee driving west toward a spring sunset.

I took a shower when I got home. No one likes a big sweaty baby.

FRIENDS AND GUTTERS

I REMOVED ANOTHER ANNOYANCE FROM MY LIFE THIS WEEK. All it took was three phone calls and an outlay of cash. While it wasn't cheap, it wasn't all that expensive.

I'd never gotten an estimate before. Each time I walked under the leaking gutter, I would look up and survey the entire length. Being a glass (and gutter) half-full kind of guy, I told myself that the channel was only leaking in three places throughout the forty-eight-foot span.

The real issue was that it leaked directly over the main door, creating enough water on the warmer days to develop a hockey rink during subsequent cold nights. I managed it through salt and scraping. In the summer, I walked around the deluge. As I've said, working around something is sometimes easier than facing it head-on, so that's what I did. I do not recommend this method.

On the opposite side of the house, there were two leaks in the gutter. On the addition to the dwelling, at the far end of Chez Cotton—housing an empty in-law apartment—the gutter sustained some horrific damage. It leaked everywhere. The good news is that it's not in an area where it matters that much, except for aesthetics. Curb appeal, I guess.

That damage was not caused by age or wear and tear but more by me and the tractor bucket. I struck it with the raised bucket while moving snow a few years ago. Yes, I lifted too high to avoid the car parked nearby. When I made a wide swing, I didn't hit the car, but I did hit the house, right in the gutter.

This year's incessant snow has led me to deal constantly with the deluges of melting roof snow. Carrying groceries into the house a few weeks ago, I got soaked trying to unlock the door. Once inside, I called my buddy, Hutch, and he gave me another guy's name. That fellow sent me to another guy, and I called him. John texted me back and asked for some photos and an estimated total length. He gave me a rough price, and we still had not spoken in person or by phone.

I have friends that are so reliable that I trust their opinions. I am blessed that way. None who makes up the inner circle would give me bad advice, so if they say the guy is good, he's good. If that guy says the gutter guy is good, he's good. He showed up with a crew and some trucks yesterday. I was off on my length estimate by about twenty feet, so the price had to be rewritten, but I expected that.

They started ripping off the old gutters when the sun started warming the roof. That meant snow became water, running down their arms and their backs while they practiced their craft. The new gutters gleam and are leak-free, something I haven't experienced for years.

This isn't about the gutters. It's about my friends. It was cold yesterday. This group of men—friends of a friend of a friend—did one heck of a job.

Long before Google reviews, Yelp, and Siri, we relied on the opinions of our friends. It's now too easy to punch up the Interweb and do our research; we feel we have exercised due diligence. But have we?

Spend the time required to pick good friends. The rest will sort itself out.

One Last Thing

I've looked down upon the sad-looking Red Wings for a couple of months. Late summer and early fall found them stowed on the floor of the backseat of my truck. They fit the bill as something that looked to have been "rode hard and put away wet."

After spending some time walking about in lighter footwear throughout the summer, I grabbed the Iron Rangers out of the truck and started wearing them again as soon as I sensed an autumn chill. They felt wonderful, but they looked dilapidated. More lightweight shoes are okay for summer sauntering, but when the trees begin to turn, my feet are happier in wrinkled leather with welt soles. For the record, I believe it's entirely psychological.

I stayed up late last night. I've been binge-watching a few shows on Netflix and got caught up in a storyline while ignoring my drooping eyelids. As I made my way toward the bedroom, out of the corner of my eye, I spotted the boots where I had kicked them off earlier. The term, there's no time like the present, overcame my forward progress toward cool sheets.

I rooted in the under-sink cupboard and found the recently purchased brown shoe cream and a can of Huberd's Shoe Grease. I've been using Huberd's for about thirty-five years.

Prying off the stepped tin top with a flat-bladed screwdriver is pleasurable in itself. No silly screw tops to spoil the nostalgia. Once I tossed the lid on the counter with a satisfying *ting*, the odor of smoky pine permeated the air around me. It's intoxicating. Pine tar and beeswax are the main ingredients; naturally, it works well.

I used to condition my footwear in front of the woodstove in my first home. I waterproofed my boots more regularly in those days. I recalled coming inside, chilled to the bone, and allowing the fire to work its magic.

Being warm is a good feeling, but the human body accepts heat with far more enthusiasm when your teeth are chattering. I miss that. I had no streaming services and few channels on cable, so my boots became my entertainment on some of those nights.

I finished up and set the rehabilitated boots on top of my propane stove so the constantly burning pilot light could slowly warm the leather overnight, allowing the pine tar and beeswax infusion to complete the process that my bare hands had started. I squirted a bit of Dawn dish detergent on my palms and scrubbed away the water repellency that was a side-effect of the hands-on application process.

I cut the lights and headed down the hall, still smelling like I had been sitting around a fire fueled with chunks of pine. I suppose, metaphorically, I'd done that.

Too often, I let the little jobs go until they become much more challenging. I'm not just talking about my scuffed-up boots. I can apply the lesson to many other things I tend to ignore.

Nope, it's not a big thing. It's just one last thing, an accomplishment, before settling into bed. I'll pay better attention for the next few months. As the last thing before sleeping, I rekindled the simple joy of keeping things in order.

September Sun's Reflections
on the Hair of a Dog

Ellie only wanted to sit amongst the fallen leaves, even as I prodded her to skitter down toward the woods line to do her business. She's a stubborn animal and tends to cause me to be frustrated when I am in a hurry to do other things.

I wasn't late. Not yet. But I wanted to get moving to my next errand. She hadn't been outside the house for about four hours because I had to complete the storm door installation that day. Her daily roving recreational opportunities fell victim to home improvements. It was the second day of her extended confinement.

Larry, a good friend and cop-retiree, helped me put in a new entry door the day before. Ellie whined from the back bedroom where I'd placed her to ensure she didn't scoot outside for a self-initiated world tour.

The forced incarceration of Ellie within the chaotic mess of tools, cracked clamshell molding, and lack of good carpentry skills was bolstered with a large sheet of cardboard to block her exit from the house. Since it was only me working on the second stage of door installation, I enjoyed her presence in the dining/living room.

As I slipped in and out of the house repeatedly, the cardboard was easy to move. It was more of a subliminal or mental barrier for the dog; she could have pushed it over without a bit of effort. Seventy-six pounds of lab/boxer could have hopped over the roadblock, but she knows the drill.

I selected a mellow string of Pandora-derived musical accompaniments to entertain us through the dump-recovered, cherry cabinet–enclosed Klipsch speakers. I think Ellie likes music but doesn't enjoy loud volume and excessive bass. Ray Lamontagne crooned "Highway to the Sun" and other selections while I leveled, caulked, and screwed the new storm door over the entrance to the open-air autumn auditorium.

Ellie kept her head still on a decorative couch pillow, following my lumbering movement with only her expressive brown eyes.

Watching a dog watch you gives you insight into their life's mindset. You can almost see their thoughts floating in cartoonish dialogue bubbles above their heads. "Is he done yet? He's not very skilled at this. We could be outside right now! I wonder if he knows that I hate Ray Lamontagne's music. How about a bit more Bad Company?"

As I cleaned up my mess while shutting and opening the new weather-defying door with a sense of pride, she bumped her nose into my leg repeatedly. "Just give me a couple of minutes, Ellie. It hasn't been that long!" I showered quickly and allowed her to scoot out through the new door. She thundered across the deck and then meandered around the dooryard, gathering information for her autobiography.

She plopped down in the grass, among the leaves, and began to stare off into the distance. I sat on the bed of my old trailer and did the same. I don't know what she was thinking, but I surmised that the sun and warm afternoon air made Ellie feel more vibrant and alive than all the good music and one-sided conversations over the last few days.

I allowed her to sit; that forced me to sit. We were still, even as Tyler Childers crooned quietly about "Shaking the

Frost" through the convenient roll-away screen of our new storm door meant to do the same. If you listen carefully, most music can fit a moment perfectly.

Ellie understood that we needed to take a few minutes of September's fleeting time to enjoy the sun's reflections on the hair of a dog.

FIDDLEHEADS

WE FED ON FURLED FRONDS FROM A FLEDGLING FERN; FAN-
tastic they were. The S.O., a female, fawned over the ferns
since arriving in Maine from further south. "Can you grab
some fiddleheads in your travels? Please. I can't get them
down here," she said. "I am waiting for the roadside sellers,
dear. None have revealed themselves, and I don't have time to
gather a mess so you can be fed your fill when you fly home."
"Fine, I'll pick some up at the grocery store, but they are five
times the price." She estimated high but wasn't too far off
the per-pound price. That's what you get when you refuse to
scour the stream banks of some waterways a little north of
home.

We either went "fiddleheading" or went on a three-day
beach vacation. For this year, she determined she would get
sand rather than mud between her toes.

Well, yesterday, she found a feed of ferns at our neighborhood grocer. She bought more than we needed, but seconds sometimes become thirds, so it was a wise decision. She
walked into the house, holding them up like she'd caught a
world-class Atlantic salmon using only a stick, string, and
hook. By the way, that's illegal unless you are only making a
written comparison. "Look at these beauties," she said.

Suddenly, apple cider vinegar became something that I
must have misplaced, at least until she looked in the lower
cupboards where we had stored a couple of liters. I stood
affirmed; no one throws out the vinegar. No one.

We were having chili, which was good. However, I pointed out that the results of chili and fiddleheads might have gastric consequences. We went ahead with the plans anyway.

Matteuccia struthiopteris—or, for those who cannot pronounce it, ostrich ferns are what Mainers (and others) call fiddleheads. They are delicious. But only when they are young and fresh.

After chili, we savored the tightly curled fronds of young ferns, their taste and texture a delightful surprise.

This is not actually surprising to us, as we are fiddlehead aficionados; you should try them if you are rooting around Maine in the early spring. If you have trouble identifying the treats, do a little research, as some people end up with the wrong kind of fern, which can leave you very unsatisfied and feeling a bit silly.

Butter is more important than apple cider vinegar, but you'll have to argue that with your housemates. I like a little vinegar, but not a lot. Salt and pepper are your friends.

Ask permission before you go rummaging around on someone else's stream bank, too. Felonious fern frolicking is frowned upon.

SUNRISE OR SUNSET?

I THINK WE ALL ENJOY A SUNSET. I'VE SAT ON ENOUGH southern beaches with gaggles of other humans waiting for the sun to drop below the horizon. Not too long ago, on the west coast of Florida, we found a chair each evening for the event. But it's the clapping that ruins it for me. Music in the background? I'm in. Applause? It feels odd to me. I've never been somewhere where people clap for the sun*rise*. While clapping seems more appropriate to celebrate a new day, another chance, a new beginning, I have never witnessed it.

A sunrise is probably a more intimate event. We rarely wake up surrounded by hundreds of people, and that's appreciated on many levels. One of the most oft-discussed coffee talks at the cabin is whether facing east or west is better. To have a full-on frontal to sundown forces one to grab a boat or a canoe, motivate out into the lake, and turn around. I only make an effort when we have company; that's not very often.

The consensus has been it's better to wake up facing the sunrise, because it's the best time for coffee. I know it's not scientific, but it's been the consistently winning vote.

We didn't select this spot for the camp, so it's not like we had a choice of sun direction when we bought it. It was chosen long before we became the caretakers. A man named Cyrus West picked this spot in the late 1800s. I don't know whether his name caused him to look toward the east from the west shore, but he did. It is far more likely that he didn't care which way he faced; like a real estate shopper in the twenty-first century, he grabbed what was available. I'm even more positive that he didn't clap at sunset or sunrise. Getting to camp was hard enough; we surmise he was too tired to clap.

Over the years, from the necessary tearing down of the old cabin, its structural underpinnings having given out from erosion and rot, to this morning in a thirty-year-old model built by a slug and his friends, the sun in your face while it's laid upon a pillow is a far better alarm clock than any ticking timepiece can provide—electrified or not.

For one thing, the sun beckons you to rise. That's not a bad thing. It forces me to rise and shine, so I don't question Cyrus's decision. If he was here, I'd shake his hand. It's so much better than applause.

ALTERNATE ROUTE

I TOOK THE LONG WAY HOME. THE ROAD, AN AVOIDED BUT available alternate route on most evenings, beckoned me with a quiet voice. It sounded remarkably like my Significant One. It was a simple question: "Can we go up Old County?" I answered yes, or the voice in my head did, without prompting, directed toward the empty seat beside me.

When she is around, we must drive by the house where she grew up at least once. It looks vastly different, but the bones and structure are familiar. If we were ever called upon to see the house before a teardown, we could positively identify it for the undertaker. "Yes, that's her," we would say.

The yard is overgrown and looks a little like 1313 Mockingbird Lane. For those who didn't watch television in the 1960s, that's the Munsters' house. It's on a slower road, and I was traveling with the windows down for nostalgia. While it was ninety-two degrees, the self-initiated thirty-seven-mile-per-hour speeds over the cracked macadam were enough to move the air through the cab, keeping me from overheating.

Excessive humidity was lacking, so I channeled my twenty-year-old self. That was back when having an air-conditioned car was only a pipe dream. I cranked Bonnie Raitt's "I Can't Make You Love Me" and slowly meandered by the old digs. Not one to gawk; it was simply the drive-by I was seeking—nothing too nosey. She wasn't with me, so braking or commenting was unnecessary.

I motored slowly up the hill that stole the last whimpering breath from the automatic transmission in my 1975 Pontiac Ventura. She had loaned me the two hundred bucks to replace it—I paid her back on the installment plan and let her use the car often, so she had skin in the game.

Yes, America, there was a time when you could buy and have a transmission installed for two hundred dollars. I got it from a junkyard and had a filthy-fingernailed mechanical genius install it in his home garage—it worked perfectly for three more years. Those were the days.

I noticed three distinct but separate scenes on that road—each Americana diorama included people chatting outside, seated in lawn chairs. I guessed their homes were not air conditioned; very few in Maine have central air. Grabbing the tail end of an evening breeze, however slight, was enough to force a designated family member out to the overhead storage in the garage to grab the nylon-webbed aluminum chairs, freshly coated with dust from the long winter.

Cotton plaid shirts, untucked, with shorts a little too tight but still cooler than jeans or work clothes, they chatted as I drove by, unfettered by the passing traffic—just talking. I saw beers, glasses filled with something that looked like iced tea, and a few indiscriminate smoke signals from cigarettes lazily burning between the fore and middle fingers of the conversers.

It was nothing and everything all at once—a snapshot of a hot night in America with the dishes left to be scrubbed a little later.

I suppose some of them might have discussed riding to Jimmy's for an ice cream cone, but not right yet, and maybe not at all—indiscriminate chatter about things that didn't matter, with snippets of tidbits that did. I ended my private tour at a stop sign that I'd rolled through hundreds of times. Back then, it was triangular and only mentioned yielding.

The off-course cruise took me only three minutes, maybe four. It was refreshing, a tour of my youth, some of which I misspent and some of which I invested wisely.

Gordon Lightfoot's "Sundown" came on next, as if planned all along. Maybe it was.

PILLOWS

THE MONTHS-LONG DELAY BETWEEN DAD'S DEATH AND the funeral service felt like a good idea. I firmly believe in making decisions based on facts, not feelings. In this case, my sibling-centric vote fell between feelings and facts. Delay seemed like a good idea.

As Friday closes in, I cradle some regret. I should have voted for closure. The premise was that more of the family could safely get to Maine in June than in February, and summertime in Maine is a much more pleasant affair. Travel to Maine comes with costs. The five of us surmised that people could make it a time for respite from their busy lives. We set it for a Friday instead of a Saturday to avoid tying someone up on one of their few available warm-weather weekends. It made sense to us at the time.

In the early stages of our new normal, one of my sisters mentioned having memory pillows created using his commonly worn shirts. I'd never heard of this, but it's a thing. The pillows' online purveyors asked for outrageous amounts of cash, which tempered the desire.

My mother had already given me a few of my dad's shirts, which I'd simply rotated into my wardrobe.

I saved one piece of now stale Wrigley's Spearmint gum—found in one shirt pocket—to be chewed sometime on Friday—when the moment feels right. He loved Wrigley's. I remember him giving me hugs when I was small, rubbing his cold cheeks and late-day stubble across my face, smelling of

Juicy Fruit intertwined with subtleties from the dissipating scent of his morning dose of Old Spice aftershave.

Dad's tastes matured, moving from Juicy Fruit gum in the sixties and seventies to the more regal scent of spearmint in his later years. However, he wouldn't have turned down a stick of the fruity flavor if you offered. I digress.

I wrote some things about my Old Man after losing him, the only form of therapy that I currently subscribe to. Several readers and commenters reiterated the mementos crafted into pillows.

Anne, a long-time reader, sent me a private message to offer her skills and service in creating the pillows. We chatted back and forth; I'll share some excerpts—I think it tells a better story. "I just thought I would offer. This is not a scam; I love your stories. Losing a parent is heartbreaking, and having something made with clothing, to me, is special. If you are interested, we could come up with a meeting destination. No, not Florida, somewhere in Maine. If you are interested, let me know. Yes, some people do things at no cost. I will be going to see my granddaughter in California all of April, but otherwise, I should be available to meet."

She told me she'd have time in late summer and that I could expect the pillows before Christmas. She was under the impression that we'd already had my dad's funeral.

I kept the bag of shirts on my counter, sometimes forgetting what the bag contained. Thus, I can give you some insight into why I keep things in view and my counter is often cluttered. When my S.O. swings by, she normally reorganizes, but she allowed the shirts to stay right where I put them, knowing their importance.

In May, I got this message from Anne:

"Hi TC, I am back from a fantastic month in California with my granddaughter. It's bittersweet, for sure. So, I am giving you some dates I have available to meet up with you during the next two weeks to collect your dad's shirts to make pillows. If one of these dates is not good for you, I can look at future dates or throw a few dates at me that are good for you. I could meet you at Exit 180 Bangor Dysarts. I hope this location works. I can also visit a friend in Bangor on the same day. I am open as far as the time of day. You pick, but not 6:00 a.m., please, LOL. I'm on retired hours."

Well, Anne and I met at a truck stop. We had a wonderful chat in a May sunbeam with the elegant rattle of diesels surrounding us. Anne spent her life working with the Maine legislature at the State House. I gave her the shirts my little sister had selected for material; Anne reiterated that she had a busy summer but promised a before-Christmas delivery date. I told her there was no rush. We hugged. I am not a hugger, but this felt appropriate.

I focused on moving forward. We moved my mom to my sister and her husband's island home, which necessitated reducing mom's possessions. Coming so soon after the downsizing of her household from two to one, there were a few struggles. Spring was tough; there's nothing more to say about that.

Anne messaged me the Monday before to let me know the pillows were done. Good things come year-round, not always at Christmas. This was her message, followed by a photo of the five completed pillows:

"Guess what?"

Anne told me that one night a week ago, she'd woken up in the middle of the night and was overcome with the feeling that she needed to finish my pillows. The following morning, she got to work, completing the pillows—they were beautifully done.

We met again at a truck stop—in Newport, Maine, this time. Anne Dumont, naturally, provided the newly sewn treasures in gift bags with tags for me to fill out. She also offered the proper amount and shade of tissue paper to top off each gift bag. Anne knew she was dealing with a man.

Maine ladies do things like this. I know, I know, there are women like Anne D. all over this great nation. They are sympathetic, empathetic, crafty, and skilled. Women make men look like layabouts—I stand by that credo.

Naturally, and as expected, Anne did not desire any compensation, but we worked through that.

No matter the price paid, it cannot be compared to the love and concern stitched with each of my father's shirts after Anne's midnight epiphany that has no earthly explanation. We talked at length about that, still surrounded by the clatter of the mechanized world and the odor of diesel and gas fumes.

She shared with me the loss of her father thirteen years ago. They had been close. She still misses him. We hugged again, but this time tighter. Dad's hugs tend to be tighter.

Memorial Drive

The sun's late afternoon trajectory, a fiery arc, pierced through the dense forest on my right. As it descended lower on the horizon, the trunks and branches, like sentinels, intermittently blocked my view, teasing the shards of light that danced and shimmered as I pressed on, maintaining a steady pace.

The Memorial Day wind, at times boisterous, whipped through the leaves and the light, infusing the scene with a sense of vitality. It animated the red, white, and blue flags proudly unfurled on poles and posts along my route, as if they, too, were paying tribute to the fallen.

The lawns seemed neatly groomed, much more so than usual, an added homage to show respect to the fallen. It might have been the one extra detail a homeowner could attend to. The additional time spent on trimming intended to show they cared about the day and, in turn, the people and the loss. For who could they tell about how they felt? Instead, they displayed green and expansive concern under their flying flags.

Route 9 is a lonely road, especially at the end of a holiday weekend, just as I like it. I sipped the coffee and reflected on the day, my automatic headlights finally giving in to dusk and the ensuing darkness that follows that golden hour. I had not attended a parade but heard the echo of the songs.

I have personally thanked vets—even on non-holiday weekends, and I've hugged a few widows, too. On this day,

I remained silent and tried to be thoughtful. I sipped the coffee, then recalled being six or seven in western Maine, scrambling with other like-minded youth to grab the hot brass shell casings as they tumbled from bolt-action rifles—the honor guard aimed high and fired blanks; seven guns, three shots each—a 21-gun salute.

I didn't know my actions were disrespectful then, but I learned later when Dad mentioned it as I emptied my pockets of the two treasures I had retrieved.

He said I should keep them and set them on my bureau, but never to do that again. I understood, and I think about it even more today. Lessons about respect can be delivered sparingly and keeping it concise and kind was how my father did it. Leave the brass alone until the public display of respect has passed.

Flags shouldn't be publicly burned, no matter what you are trying to say. I'll stick with the philosophy. He didn't have to tell me that; I feel that in my bones. Flags should be flown, and the lawn trimmed. People died so you could burn it, yes, technically. But letting it fly says so much more about why you can say and do what you want almost every day of the year.

After all, it's not about you. It's about all of us. But it's primarily about those who weren't here for the ride home on Memorial Day.

Ernie Is My Co-Pilot

I LIKE TO THINK OF MYSELF AS SOMEONE WHO NOTICES THE little details that make up the big picture. I don't claim to have been the best detective, but I was pretty good.

I wasn't a collector of physical evidence. I was more of a mouthpiece. A conversationalist. An interviewer. I did depend on good evidence techs to gather the clues that made future conversations with suspects more focused and fruitful.

Television shows that are popular right now tend to praise crime scene investigators. I can't stand watching any of them. Mainly because I know that fiction makes seeking the truth seem so exciting; it's not.

The techs that I worked with never looked like those on the television, and they were much more snarky. None of them got into shootouts, car chases, or were involved in the physical arrest of suspects. They were too busy doing the arduous work that made them happy. However, I also know, if television productions were to show an actual investigation from beginning to end, no one would watch it.

This is just a story about a well-loved and well-used item in my world—a quilted packing blanket.

The protective blanket became mine well over twenty years ago. I am making rough estimates, so it may very well have been with me for twenty-five years. I used it to move from my first house to my current home, and that was in 2001. It's been with me on camping trips as a sleeping pad, covered furniture in the back of my truck, used in other people's trucks, and has been utilized as a makeshift bed by three of my dogs, one of whom slept on it this past weekend at camp.

I've loaned it out to other people, including my son. When he moved north a couple of years ago, he took it and kept it for a considerable amount of time. I always get it back, fold it up, and stow it somewhere in the truck. I've become attached to it, but this past weekend I made a shocking discovery.

There are Muppet characters emblazoned all over the darn thing. Not once, until pulling it out of the truck this weekend, did I ever notice the image of Ernie, the figure of Bert, or the slogan that says, "The Joy of Cookies."

I stood at the tailgate, after shaking out the gravel, and stared, stupefied. I had completely missed the whimsical characters all over my pride and joy of a packing blanket. No one else has ever mentioned it to me, and I have lent it to dozens of people. Sure, I have observed that the blanket presents many of the primary colors, but I never noticed the letters of the alphabet or the shoeprints that look remarkably like the soles of Ernie's big sneakers.

I stood for a few minutes looking over the intricacies and details of something I have loved for many other reasons. Now, I have a reason to love it even more. If someone had been watching me, I believe they might have seen a bit of moisture well up in my eyes. I wiped it away with the cuff of my dirty shirt, cautiously looking around to make sure no one had caught me in my moment of Muppet mindfulness. Those little rascals have been riding around with me for a very long time.

I snapped a photo, then folded my blanket and put it back in a location more toward the front of the bed, way up under the tonneau cover. Suddenly, I wanted to take better care of my longtime companion of softness and safety.

The Muppet moment (or three) confirmed my belief that we don't pay close enough attention to the things—maybe the people, too—who are close to us. Hurrying to fold things up way too fast, we all miss the little nuances of life. Is it because we all want to get on to the next big thing?

We all need to slow down and look for the characters hiding within the primary colors all around us.

Have we missed the simple joy of cookies? I did, and it was my blanket.

A Tale of Two American Dreams (and Ninjas)

I drove right by the manifestation of the American dream, and I immediately kicked myself for passing it by. I regretted my dismissiveness for over two miles and half of a country song that I can't recall right now.

I was happily haunted by the hopefulness I saw in his face as he tried to make the sale. I couldn't read the sign he was holding up as I passed him at twenty-eight miles per hour. No electronic device could have tracked me any better than the eyes of that little rascal.

It was clear that he was selling something cool and refreshing to drink, but it was a little after six o'clock in the evening, and I wasn't thirsty. I just wanted to get home, feed the dog, and re-heat something for dinner.

My mind provides flashbacks that are unrelenting visitors, and, for about a mile, I recalled selling red berry Kool-Aid with my best buddy, Todd. We needed fifty cents each in order to make entry into a local Revolutionary War history museum for a tour. Yes, it was a long time ago, but certainly well past 1776.

It took us over two hours—as I recall—to raise the one dollar. But upon the completion of our tiny and underfunded enterprise, we did get a personal tour by the in-house curator before the place closed for the day. Looking back, I am pretty sure that my mom and dad would have fronted us the money, but it was a good feeling to be independent businessmen selling Kool-Aid for ten cents per Styrofoam cup.

Back to my present-day dilemma. My right foot hovered over the brake pedal at several locations that provided me an ample opportunity to turn around, but I kept going. I wasn't thirsty, not for a drink. What I was thirsty for was a sip from the crumpled Styrofoam cup of the America I grew up in. I hit the left blinker and took a side street that would lead me back to the lad who was clearly placed there, at that very moment, so that I might once again taste the small and seemingly insignificant segment of a life I had once lived.

He was kind and polite when I asked his name. I guessed his age correctly; I am pretty good at that. His presentation was on point, and he provided hand sanitizer for his patrons. I wanted to get inside his head. Not too deep, mind you, but just far enough so that I could get an idea about the long-term plans of this young man named Alex.

"Is there anything specific you are hoping to buy with the proceeds of your sales?"

"A Lego set," he said.

"Which one?" I asked.

"Ninjas," he said.

"Ahhhhh!" I said.

It was clear to me who drove this well-executed plan of action. Ninjas. I should have guessed. It all made sense. "I'd like a cup of iced tea."

Alex swiftly transitioned from salesman to server. The ice cubes—suspended in the tea—clicked, clacked, and collided as they rushed toward the cup. Some were allowed to escape from the spout of the pitcher. It was a masterful business strategy; it allowed the customer's concoction to remain cool if they needed to mobilize and move on after the deal was done.

How many pitchers have you sold today?"

"I think, eight? I'm not sure. This is my last one." This was fortuitous. I had arrived just in time—for both of us.

"I have a lot of respect for you, out here, working late. I appreciate it. I want you to know that, Alex." He smirked but remained silent. I slid the only folding money I had into his jar. It was much more than the price on the sign, but we are smack dab in an inflationary period. I was amazed by the generosity of those who came before me. His cash jar was overflowing with bills in denominations that appeared to be much larger than his very reasonable—one dollar—asking price. The kid was killing it.

It was obvious that all of us were buying something more than a cup of iced tea. It was a veritable buy one, get one free event. The second item in the transaction—free to all of us who had stopped by—wasn't meant to quench our physical thirst. We stopped for something more, and I bet all who stood there long enough walked away with exactly what they were looking for.

I told him it was delicious, with just the right amount of ice. He smiled the subdued smile that a boy his age should be smiling when contemplating the compliment of an odd stranger asking far too many questions.

I asked if he would mind if I took his photo. Maybe I could help him advertise a bit if his venture ever expanded. He said, "Okay."

I didn't sense elation in his demeanor; I wasn't his highest paying customer. I did, however, sense a bit of his satisfaction in the sale as we both headed toward our separate suppers. I know, because I have felt that same satisfaction during my own renditions of the American dream.

The following day, I stopped by and spoke to the pleasant parents of Alex. I introduced myself, and I told them of our encounter. I let them know that I had written something I wanted to share on my blog, and maybe on the Bangor Police page. I inquired about using the photo I had taken as I knew there were some folks who might find it to be intrusive, and you cannot be too careful. Mom said that she had seen me take the photo from her window seat at the house. In her mind, she wondered why I might have done that, but I guess I appeared to be a decent human with no bad intentions. I also made sure they were okay with me sharing their son's first name. Then I asked permission from Alex himself. I was cleared to share those tidbits, and his photo. We had a nice visit. As for the Lego Ninjago purchase, Mom and Dad are urging Alex to open a bank account first, and then—together—they will review the costs associated with an investment in Ninjagos. You know, good parents helping the lad move through his newfound wealth in a thoughtful way. Step two of the American dream—personified by concerned and caring overseers. Could any of us have made it without a little of that?

WONDERING

TONIGHT, I BEGAN TO WONDER WHEN ELLIE TRANSITIONED from young to old. Her frosted tips have spread around a bit. I first saw the gray in her muzzle, then in her eyebrows. Suddenly, the silver highlights were everywhere.

At night, she sits beside me on the couch. Sometimes remaining completely still and staring for over an hour. She can sleep while sitting up, and she does it quite regularly. It's odd to have a dog looking over your shoulder when you are writing, but she never speaks to me about grammatical errors. I can deal with her choice of seating positions.

The way she plants herself on the couch makes me laugh. I think that's why we stay together. Her mom was a pure boxer dog and spent much of her time sitting with her master—upright—in a chair in their mid-coast farmhouse living room. Ellie must come by the strange positioning naturally.

Her dad was a chocolate lab whose hobbies included more amatory pursuits. He was able to lift the latch of the door to Mom's room—with his snout—when the time came to consummate their illicit love affair. It seems that's how our Ellie came to be.

When we selected her from the way-back of a Volvo 240 wagon, her pet-mom advised us that she didn't want to take any money for her. She had advertised the box-a-dor puppies for the sum of two-hundred-and-fifty dollars. She said she would refund the entire sum when I provided to her the medical records proving that Ellie had been spayed. I paid her the money but never asked for a refund once Ellie had her procedure.

Ellie held a lot of promise. Initially, I felt she was far more trainable. I mean, she *is* trainable, but I am not patient enough to get by her stubborn streak. I suppose I'm not all that trainable. We stuck with the basics. Come when I call, don't poop in the house, get off the bed when I tell you to, don't bite the pleasant people who stop by the house or camp. Oh, and guard the truck so that I can leave tools and things lying around on the seats while forgetting to put the windows up when I go in some joint for coffee and pie.

She's been a stellar performer. Oh, she does other things—sits, stays, shakes, and catches treats like a boss.

I only wanted a dog to be a dog. She's got it down pat. Sure, I have to beep the horn of the truck—sometimes— to get her to come back from her walkabouts at the lake. Usually, I slam the door a couple of times before reaching for the horn. The sound of doors slamming will usually bring her in if she is within shouting distance. Yes, it does cause you to shake your head in wonder when shouting her name didn't work in the first place; I know I can holler louder than the sound of a door slamming.

One of her annoying traits is that she peeps. She cries really. Whenever there is some urgent and unknown angst, she whimpers, peeps, cries, and moans. Her noises can be incredibly off-putting, but what are you going to do? We all have flaws.

When she is in, she wants to be out. When she is resting, she'd rather be running, and when she's eating, don't get between her and the bowl. When she growls, listen to her.

When she stares and groans in unison, it's time to go out-side. She is incredibly proud of her record of *never* having an accident inside the house, not even once since showing up when she was only eight weeks old. That's six years of savings in paper towels alone.

A few weeks ago, Ellie came up lame after four straight hours of playing with an energetic five-month-old puppy. She limped for a day, but she came out of it. Telling her to slow down would be useless, and she is too stubborn to recall that she is not a puppy anymore.

I guess the key to making her slow down is to model the behavior for her. I'll just sit on the couch and write some stuff. She will sit and stare. Tonight, *she's* probably wondering when I transitioned from young to old.

Odd Man Out

Ellie is having withdrawals from a few weeks with the Significant One. She only sleeps in the SO's chair for a couple of days immediately following the frequent early morning—wheels-up—departures. She then returns to her standard sleeping couch or the bay window, I suppose after the scent of a woman has left the building.

It seems that while you may think that I am Ellie's person, Ellie feels otherwise. The two of them share a little of the "ladies stick together" attitude. It was the Significant One who selected Ellie from the way-back of that Volvo 240. I was focused on Ellie's bigger brother, Tyler. Tyler was white with a black patch around his eye. The SO was having none of that.

Ellie was the shy one in the car. All nine of her siblings were running her over. The lovely lady who brought all the puppies to Belfast said we could pick out any one of them— except Tyler. She and her husband had decided to keep him on the farm. With that, Ellie came home. Yup, I did all the late-night walks, the feeding, the failed training at keeping her from becoming boorish and annoying—all me. Still, when mama comes home, Ellie is all about her.

When the SO is home, Ellie sleeps well past the regularly utilized timetable that she employs every other day to force me to rise and shine. I get up and head to my writing space without the resonant clicking of claws on the hardwood behind me. Ellie waits for her pal to get up; they come out, stretching and yawning, together. Ladies can be like that.

The minute the two roller bags get dragged out to the landing for another trip to the other world, Ellie goes on high alert. She hates the early morning departures, and she stands in the bay window to help us visualize her displeasure as we drive out of the yard. Two of us leave, only one of us returns. Ellie gets a little depressed and sleeps a lot for a day or so after that—poor girl.

Once the minor moving and mayhem settles, I find Ellie back in the chair. I never sit there, and I'm not sure that Ellie would let me. She's there today. On and off, she will utilize the old wingback. Give her some time. She will come out of it. The chair will then remain empty until the SO's next visit to the Jagged Edge.

It'll be three or four weeks, and we will start this whole cycle again. Ladies can be like that.

Keeping Our Boats Afloat

The phone buzzed across the dusty surface of my nightstand last night. I generally avoid looking at texts during the witching hour, but my current agenda includes answering specific inquiries that I have made through the magic of electronic communication. I've been perusing Facebook Marketplace.

I was trying to buy another old aluminum boat. The craft I purchased last year—to replace the one I sold last year—is far too shallow in depth for the safekeeping of cargo that I take aboard. The freight is typically just an old black dog and me, but my granddaughter enjoys catching fish when she comes to the lake, so I'm more aware of safety now.

To add some clarity to my admission, most of my aluminum boats have leaked more than I liked. I don't spend a lot on them, and it's kind of a hobby of mine to be perpetually trading up to something that seems slightly better. Usually, they are just about the same, but you don't lose much money selling and buying disheveled and dented aluminum boats.

So, I picked up, hoping that the fuzzy-faced, camo-clad character had accepted my offer on the larger modified-v hull. It sported a dull, dead-grass-green paint job that would blend in with my soon-to-be publicly displayed disappearing act. I looked at the screen; it wasn't my boat connection guy.

Him: "Is this Tim Cotton?" I recognized the name on the account as someone I hadn't seen in at least twenty-five years.

Me: "Yes, how are you?"

Him: "Hey, brother, I'm doing pretty amazing. I seen a post with your name at the bottom of it, and I was like, man, I was so thankful for what a great guy you are. I still remember you used to bring me candy bars and s#*t. I come a long way from those days. . . . I know you have kids now, and you know, it just struck a chord with me how you went above and beyond what most people would."

We last talked when the man was nine or ten, and I clearly remembered him from many not-so-positive interactions. He is featured in my first book, *The Detective in the Dooryard*, in an essay called "The Kid from the Trailer Park."

I answered the text, of course. You can't ignore memories that vividly reveal themselves in bold words from a dimly lit screen. I think about many of the kids I've met over the years. Their stories haunt me on some days. I usually push it out of my mind by searching for cheap aluminum boats that I don't need. I clickity-clicked back to him—

"I'm so glad that I made some impact. It means a lot that you noticed. I'm so happy that you are doing well. Where are you living now?"

"I'm in Tennessee. Telecommunications engineer now. I mean, really, what I've come from gave me a lot of perspective that most wouldn't have."

"That is so great! I think of you often. I always knew you had it in you. You came up with some tough circumstances. I'm proud of what you have become."

"For sure. But I'm proud of where I am. I still have my own struggles. It's called life. LOL, it's not all peaches. But I definitely look at things differently. I try to learn from my mistakes now. I'm human. But having a leader like you helped me through. I didn't know it until later in life. But man, it is so good to hear from somebody such as yourself. Know that you had such a big impact on my life when I was much younger. I definitely gave you a run for your money, but luckily, that's not the case anymore."

"I always knew you could pull it off. It sounds like you did. That's pretty great to hear as I get close to retirement this summer. Makes me happy to hear from you. Thanks for reaching out. It means so much to me!"

"Yes, Tim. You will enjoy that retirement, brother. Because I can assure you that you've earned it . . . and I know the type of impact you made on me. That's the same interaction that you had with everybody you met. So, you left your mark on this world, Tim. I can assure you that everybody knows it. So, again, thank you very much!"

"Thanks. If you get up to Maine, drop me a line. I'd love to buy you a coffee and hear the rest of the story. Be well, my friend."

And with that, I plugged my phone back in and slid it back across the nightstand.

I slept well. I've not heard from the camo-clad man with the dull, dead-grass-green boat. My offer was probably a bit low.

The Quilt Lady: Don't Let Her Fool You

My dealer is a diminutive lady who has an addiction of her own; she appears to be overrun with product. I'm merely the means to an end.

It's not something that I am proud of, either; men don't admit habits like this one. I'm sure my T-levels are reasonable; I still look longingly at muscle cars, power tools, and pickup trucks built before plastic-wrapped bumpers were considered stylish upgrades.

Okay, I'll admit that driving a Plymouth Valiant with a slant-six wouldn't bother me a bit. The term "Valiant" certainly doesn't dredge up memories of big wins on straight stretches of road. But reasonable gas mileage and the constant ticking of the iron-blocked Chrysler Corporation's bread-and-butter powerplant makes me misty for the days when you had to borrow your aunt's car for date night. Sure, it was a four-door, but double-dating could cut expenses in half. I miss the sound of the parking pin clicking comfortably home—loudly— inside the sloppy transmission when you threw it into park just a bit before coming to a complete stop.

The thing is, I like quilts. There, I said it. I like quilts.

Just for the record, I like Clint Eastwood's spaghetti westerns too. I think it's essential that everyone knows that.

It all started at an early age, but the addiction took hold after taking ownership of the camp in the woods. Several old quilts came with the dilapidated cedar-shingled hovel.

It was torn down and replaced, but the musty, frayed quilts were salvaged.

They were tattered and shabby from years of use. My lady quilt dealer fixed one of them up the best she could. She usually downplays her work in a most self-deprecating way. "I did what I could, but it's not perfect. The material is so old that the thread just won't hold. It's usable if you are careful. I'm sorry I couldn't do better."

The thing is, it was much better.

My dealer gifted me the most backwoods-chic handmade quilt at Christmas a few months later. It's camouflage, and I think tiny whitetail deer prints are on the other side. I keep it at camp for naps. I use it to cover my feet late in the fall—before the woodstove fire amps up, and after tromping across the frigid floor to grab another mug of coffee.

She gave me a quilt that she felt wasn't up to her standards the very next year. She cut it in half and restitched the edges so that two people could use the same quilt while sitting—or lying—in different locations. I think there is a wool army blanket used as stuffing between the patchwork. It's marvelous.

I'm not sure if it's an actual army blanket, but the term needed to be added for a touch of masculinity; this is hard for me.

Once they get you hooked, kind and timid quilt ladies sometimes call, late at night, to advise you that they have a quilt that you might like. This past summer, she lured me to her home and approved me for a quick rummage through a colossal basket mounded with her handiwork. She let me pick one out. She priced it low, most likely to keep me coming back.

That wool quilt came with a matching miniature quilt intended as a lap blanket. It's warm, heavy, and a welcome comfort when I turn down the heat during late winter nights at Chez Timmay. She has me economizing for future quilt purchases; this is what dealers force you to do.

Things got pretty intense one Wednesday night. She had reverted to social media for making contact. She embraced technology to keep me interested; my Messenger app lit up. I turned the screen away from the Significant One, who is currently visiting. I don't want her to catch on.

"Wanna buy a wool quilt for camp?"

"Maybe. I don't need it. But I like them. Is it attractive. Lol."

"Ok, thought I'd check. Hope all is well."

"Well, you didn't answer my question. Lol."

"Oh, it's beautiful. I can show it to you in 2 minutes. I'm in . . ."

As you can see she is clearly up to no good. I've turned into her best customer. The thing is, she is heavily discounting the quilts to keep me coming back.

She turned out her Kia's lights the minute she pulled into the driveway; she was so coy. I didn't hear her coming up the steps. I stowed the dog in the bathroom to keep her from barking. Silent visits from the quilt lady will surely get the neighbors talking.

This particular quilt is made from parcels of wool taken from multiple lady-type sports jackets that she has cut up since she retired last summer. She's even left in some of the pockets; I remarked that those pockets are good places to hold screws, nails, or even cigarettes. I don't smoke, but I blurted it out, hoping she wouldn't judge me. I'll use the pockets to store late-night snacks; she doesn't need to know. I'm sure I'll need professional help at some point. I took TQL's photo with my latest acquisition. I can at least leave it out on the counter for use by investigators when they see my bank account is empty before they stop by the house to see if I am okay.

They'll probably find me wrapped in a quilt. I hope someone checks my pulse before rolling me out the door to take me to rehab; there's a good chance that I'm only warmly napping.

JUST A BOOST

I ONLY NEEDED A BOOST—JUST A LITTLE. BUT MOST OF THE time, it's enough.

The tiny ladder came to me by happenstance—luck, more or less. I'll take some credit for the find, but only because I watch the ditches and wood lines while I drive.

Way down in the grass on Route 202, a summer's day, probably around 1990, maybe 1991—there it was. It could have flown off the top of a van. More than likely, though, it fell out of the open tailgate of a pickup truck.

The first time I saw it, I kept driving. I had someplace to be, as I recall. The second time, on the way home, I spotted it again. Still, I kept driving. I'd looked for it, but it appeared so small, I believed it must be broken, the remains of what once certainly had been a very lovely wooden stepladder.

Two or three days later, I ran by the ladder. Yes, I used to run every day. Like I said, it was a long time ago. I'd passed by enough. It was time. I slowed my jog to a snail's pace to check it out. It wasn't bent or broken. The ladder was tiny, just as the fine folks at the Werner ladder company had intended. I stood it up to its full height. If someone lost it, they probably drove by every day. I wanted to take it home, but it was about two miles from the house. Running down the roadside, sweaty, carrying a miniature ladder didn't appeal to me. It was a handy size; cute, almost.

During a Werner meeting, someone probably said, "All ladders don't have to be tall; there are those times that you merely need a boost." I picture those around the elongated wooden table—maybe during the monthly new product gatherings—agreeing. Looking right and left, most nodded in agreement. It makes sense. The boss steepled his hands together, maybe tapping his top lip as he looked pensive for a minute. Finally, he looked up and said, "Let's make one. Joe, you're in charge of the design. Bill, you get this into production. Let's get some lunch." I digress.

A few days later, I drove slowly toward the ladder. Sure to be out of the traffic flow, I kept to the far right on the gravel-strewn shoulder. I saw it, barely standing above the late summer grass. I picked up the ladder, feeling I had done due diligence, leaving enough time between the finders and the keepers. I took it home.

It wasn't long after that when my home ownership mentor, Dan, aided me in putting in a couple of outlets. We didn't need the ladder; we were both on our knees. Dan showed me how to do almost everything that needed doing to an old house. Plumbing, wiring, basement concrete repairs; the list is endless. Sometimes, a fellow needs a boost.

Shortly after that, the miniature ladder debuted in the 1860s cape. I put a light kit on a ceiling fan. Low ceilings made a tall ladder unnecessary; I'm glad I had it. When we moved to a newer house with similar issues, the ladder was perfect for all sorts of boosting needs. It's a bit rickety but holds well over the designated weight limit. I can attest to that. I've even defied the maximum height limitations.

Yup, I've had to stand on the top step. It's a no-no. The folks at Werner were specific. It's all there, clearly printed on the label. We lost an outside motion light during the recent prolonged power outage. I have no idea how it affected the motion sensor, but it no longer sensed motion. The light came on only if I flicked the indoor switch thirty or forty times. Even then, it would only stay on for a moment.

I picked up a new light and installed it yesterday in light rain. I looked around for a kitchen stool used to get into the cupboards, but I must have misplaced it the last time I reached for the extra cans of Campbell's tomato soup—I was on a toasted cheese kick for a couple of days. I shuffled to the cellar to grab my trusty miniature ladder. One foot, ten inches, was all that was required. The wiring was simple.

My instructor is long gone from this earth. He's a guy I think about almost monthly when I fix something without needing to call someone else. I will take credit for being observant because that was necessary for my trade—the ladder was fair game. I learned almost everything else from someone else.

Often, you only need a boost—just a little. Most of the time, it's enough.

SNEAKERS

MY DAD TOLD ME A FEW STORIES ABOUT TRUDGING TO school. That's what dads born before 1945 tended to do. He told me a few times he wore sneakers year-round through the western Maine winters.

He explained he had to wear thicker socks in cold weather. Any kid worth his salt on the baseball diamond had worn holes in the canvas of their sneakers before returning to school in September.

I remember cheap sneakers getting decimated within weeks of purchase. You kept wearing them, but I was lucky because I had boots in the winter.

The commonly shared tale about the trip to the schoolhouse being an uphill slog both ways, with snow regularly making an appearance, was communicated to most kids born in the sixties. You see it referenced on social media but usually shaded negatively. I believe it was darn good information.

Then, we wait for the comments to light up with the favored derogatory catchphrase, "Okay, we've heard it before, Boomer." I don't scold them; I shake my head, for listening to the stories and keeping them in mind will make you a more well-rounded individual.

I received my history lessons through school textbooks, word of mouth, and perusing twelve-year-old encyclopedias that smelled like the neighbor's damp basement.

Everyone's cellar was wet when I grew up, and no one could afford to buy a new set of encyclopedias except the middle school librarian on fat budget years. Dry basements are relatively new to Maine; don't take a dry basement for granted.

I didn't live in any house without a stacked stone foundation and dirt-floor basement until 1999. In the spring, one of my chores was ensuring the actively flowing stream didn't overrun the arrangement of rocks meant to keep it relatively contained until it exited the opposite side of the house.

Oh, and the mold didn't kill us. Not yet anyway. So shut up about that.

Whenever I did a research project, the one encyclopedia I was looking for would be missing because smarter kids who were definitely on a path to a college education showed up early and stayed late; they tended to grab the reference books labeled with vowels. I adapted, being perpetually behind the eight-ball; I had no choice but to select the always-remaining X-Y-Z edition.

I must have written at least two papers on the xylophone's influence on music of the seventies. Refer now to Starbuck's "Moonlight." It features a delightful xylophone solo about mid-song. It feels right.

I referenced the song and writers correctly in the footnotes, as my sister in high school showed me. Remember, there was a time before Google—you had to ask your sister.

Waiting until the night before the due date was my mantra—and it still is. There's a story for your kids: show up early so you don't end up like that Cotton kid.

As shared, the stories, all with a different twist, were told to teach us resilience and self-confidence and to get us to shut up when we complained that our brother used the last of the Tang or had been in the bathroom too long.

You might have to look up Tang, but it's easy. You have Google.

The stories about darker times are good to recall because similar times will sooner or later revisit us. Don't ignore the harbingers.

Why did I think about my dad's ripped sneakers trudging through western Maine snow? Good question.

I was loading my truck to head to the dump the other morning. Snow that fell overnight melted in the unseasonably warm spring sunshine (a blessing). When I opened my tailgate, about a gallon of water from the tonneau cover cascaded directly onto the tops of my sneakers. They happen to be waterproof.

I purchased my first waterproof sneakers when I had enough of frequent morning dew soaking through my aging, breathable sneakers. The modern-day textiles facilitated my socks getting soaked within the two steps walking across my lawn. I got sick of it, looked these up, and ordered them.

First-world problems, for sure.

I looked down at my sneakers, shedding water like the back of a frog, and I thought about my dad's cold feet. He wasn't complaining about it, mind you. Dad merely told me those things to enlighten me, causing me to reconsider that things can always be worse.

I went all day with dry feet. But I'd had a heads-up about it. And I listened. We all should.

That's all I've got besides warm, dry feet.

SLEEPING SOUNDLY

SHE DROPPED THE TINY HUMAN RIGHT IN OUR LAPS. HE's my grandson, but it's been over five years since I changed a diaper on anything this small. The first official babysitting duties were underway.

My daughter-in-love gave me a rundown on the milk bottle. These are much more technical now. The cap and nipple break down into four separate pieces, and there's a baffle to prevent the rascal from ingesting air and burping like a trucker who just finished the Fifth Wheel steak and mashed potato special.

The formula left behind on the counter came from goats, but the boy likes it. Heck, I like goats.

The holding and nurturing came more naturally after ensuring my wristwatch would not scratch his little melon when I moved and cautiously practiced hand-to-hand, side-to-side transitions without losing traction on that all-important neck support. You can learn a lot from a mother. I do pay attention when mothers hold their children. I'll never be as smooth or polished, but I make it work.

The diapering came back to me, and he withheld spraying his Gramps until later. There was a time when I thought his father might become a firefighter during his earliest years; he loved to hose me down.

The best part of our afternoon was watching him try to fall asleep. He fought the urges, trying his darndest to keep his eyes open. An infant, or puppy, failing to hold off a nap is one of the most calming things I have ever witnessed. I should have recorded it to watch it again at 2:00 a.m., while trying to return to a slumber of my own.

Once I figured out how to place him in the little crib, he gave up on sleep. Instead, he just talked to himself in the back bedroom. His language is foreign to me, but it sounded friendly and reassuring. As a faulty human, it was satisfying enough that my care provided him with comfort and security, allowing him to relax and chat about whatever topic crossed his mind.

We left the door ajar so that we could listen. He carried on for an hour.

When his mama arrived, she placed him in his car nest. He looked up at her adoringly. Suddenly, without even the warning of a blinking eye, sleep settled over him like a warm velvet blanket.

That's what he wanted—the same thing we all want— the ability to feel so safe that we can sleep soundly.

GOODBYE TO JANUARY

I WAS OUT OF WORDS FOR THE MOMENT. IF WINTER WERE A fishing reel, someone set the drag two notches past perfect.

It was an expected doldrum. It usually hits me before February pulls into her parking space. I'm happy to help January pack up its black Samsonite full of moth-chewed sweaters and socks with holes near the little toe—very annoying.

February is a brighter houseguest. February smiles more. I have lots of friends who complain about February. I see their point. She can bring some freezing weather, but February also comes equipped with a better heater. The sun crawls a little higher into the sky. Who can complain about that? Oh, someone will, for sure.

Snowbanks start to honeycomb and crystalize within a few weeks under the more powerful sunbeams. Water drips from icy enclaves in the roof gutters, creating comforting drops from temporary glaciers.

There would be more sun on our faces. I'd written before and would write again—the warm sun on my face always makes me feel better. Squinting to see a distant beacon—like June—is the perfect excuse for the laugh lines around my eyes. You can refer to them as wrinkles, but I know better.

February initially brings frigid air, but later in the month she will surprise us with a temporary thaw. It always happens. Well, only sometimes, but where is the fun in a guarantee?

The Three-Degree Sneak

When the thermometer indicates three degrees, I know Ellie won't be gone long during her morning constitutional. Cold doesn't bother her regularly, but the frozen, crusty snow tingles her toe pads a modicum more when she leaves the comfort of cozy carpeting.

She's a sneak. Even if I don't step outside with her, I can track her progress around the yard by watching the reflection of the motion lights through various house windows. She must know I slack off in my concern when it gets colder.

This morning, the motion light at the house's far end kicked on, indicating that she was heading in a direction where my access was limited—her next stop was fifteen acres of forest and possibly some homes on the other side. There are dogs there, and she hears them at night. During cold, clear weather, their voices carry.

When Ellie heard me walk out on the deck, she quickly turned to come back. She doesn't even wait for me to speak sharply. She hears me because the noise of the deck boards popping in the cold air is shocking, especially when this thundering lump of man flesh takes a few quick steps to aid in the re-settlement of the pressure-treated lumber loosened by the cold dryness.

I watched her black buttocks spin around, her eyes reflecting the luminescence of excessive LED lighting, making her appear to be a snow demon preparing to gather a few cold souls.

She looks sweeter and more manageable when she pads up the stairs to my deck of overwatch. Her brown eyes averted away from me to show that she was sorry for seeking the sinful companionship of the unknown hounds on the other side of the hardwoods. It could also be that I appeared to be a half-naked madman—no one wants to see that.

She expected a scolding, but it was too cold to stand in my boxers, and the morning light was rising so that passersby might notice a man wearing merely Hanes and Crocs giving his dog the devil for trying to make a break for social reasons.

I tossed her a biscuit and filled her bowl with her love language. I believe she was surprised not to be rebuked for the attempted break.

What kind of dog would I have raised if she had not tried to meet her neighbors?

The Bees from Next Door

Bright sunny skies, warm breezes, and smiles were on tap for Happy Hour at Chez Ellie. I shut down all the heat sources in the house, opened windows, and swiped right on the sliding window of the screen door that leads to the back deck, saying a hearty *yes* to cross ventilation. We only refer to it as happy hour because we were happy; we had coffee.

The bees came out, too. While I frantically typed many words that later were cut by brutal attrition, I noted that the security camera on the front porch alerted me to the flying intruders.

Many hives are nearby, and I am constantly in the company of beautiful honeybees. We both emerge when the weather is reasonable, but I couldn't go outside to recreate yesterday. On the other hand, they take every opportunity to be productive. I have a lot of respect for bees. None of them ask to work from home, and they rarely vacation somewhere warmer. Rise and shine is undoubtedly inscribed on a plaque hanging near their hive's exit.

On cooler days, they land in sunbeams nearby, sitting and enjoying it like I do. They could be alarmed that flowers aren't blooming, but this year the weather confuses all of us.

Last autumn, many of them stopped by when I was working in the yard or cleaning out my truck. A few landed on my hands, taking a break from work. They showed no animosity to me, and I appreciated looking at them closely. I could hold them up to my face to look directly into theirs. It's remarkable. I've been stung many times, but only by wasps and hornets.

These bees give off a gentle vibe, and I imagine they are only here to make peace and maybe get verbal permission to raid my mother's flower garden. My mom has since moved, and her flowers thrive, but not as beautifully as when she was around tending to them daily, overseeing them for growth and overcrowding. The bees miss her, I am sure.

The bees were channeling my youth, when I would head to my friend's house and knock loudly to inquire about taking a bike ride or walking to the school playground to smash the tetherball for a few minutes.

Bees don't make fists, so knocking was out. Instead, they buzzed the cameras, setting off the sensor so I knew they were kicking off their early spring happy hour.

And yes, it's spring. It is not on your calendar, but March 1 is what the meteorologists go by. If we entertain twenty minutes out of every half hour of news programming for them to tell us it's cloudy, we should trust them regarding the official seasons.

Enjoy your day. If the bees show up today, I will go outside. I owe them that much.

A Soft Tap with a Firm Grip

Tonight, as it often does, the softer hands of grief tapped me on the shoulder while I was driving into the sunset.

I'd frequently go to see my dad and mom on nights precisely like this. After an ice cream, I'd swing in for a dooryard visit. A ten-minute hello to catch up, but nothing riveting would be said. We'd visit for a few, talk about the Red Sox on the television, and then I'd be gone, feeling satisfied that all was right in the world.

He'd never forget to ask how my dog was doing before the conversation tapered off. Sometimes, he'd ask about two dogs in the early years when I had more patience and didn't mind sharing a bed with a lab, a setter, and the Significant One.

"How's Jack and Grace?"

"Good," I'd say.

"I stopped the other day, and ol' Jack acted like he would come through the window. I stuck my hand in the door, and as soon as he sniffed a little, he let me in." Dad would laugh. He loved tough dogs who didn't bite him.

I never locked my door. During some of those years, I patrolled the town I lived in; I drove by my house thirty times a day, able to see if there was a problem. And, truthfully, Jack would have taken someone's arm off; there was no question. But not Dad's arm; nope, he smelled like family.

Tonight, the summer atmosphere surrounded me in glorious warmth, with a touch of a breeze coming through the window. Oh, and Spandau Ballet on "80s on 8." I am not a Spandau Ballet fan, but I played "True" in the early 80s while working on the radio—before I was a cop.

The specific song only matters because when played, its melody gives a nod to hidden thoughts waiting for the perfect song to come out and dance back through time.

I drive the same roads I've always driven. My parents lived less than one and a half miles away, so swinging by wasn't a chore. It was expected and embraced. It was a simple left turn into a driveway. He was always there.

The song, the breeze, and my mind melded into a trifecta of memories, bouncing from one summer to the next. Soon, autumn will do the same thing to me. I'll probably smell pungent wood smoke on a cold October night; grief will visit again, I hope, with a softer tap on the shoulder and a song that I like better.

I Can't See Them,
But I Can Hear Them Walking

My ant stopped by with friends. She's a pest.

Before you get all worked up over the spelling of "ant," go back to memorizing your *Chicago Manual of Style*—I have no aunts in the area.

It was a summer for ants on the Jagged Edge, and it was dry for a spell. I thought I had won the war by using a bit of peppermint and some white vinegar and keeping all the food closed up tightly, but I still captured and killed a couple per day.

For some reason withheld from me, they gathered last night, just waiting for me to get up. Yup, they were carpenters—several wore tool belts. They'd only just begun.

There were a few in the bathroom near the shower and about fifty reinforcements waiting at the transition between the porch and the tiny sitting area where I do most of my writing. I turned out the light to avoid upsetting them and rummaged through the various cans of wasp spray, ant traps, bug repellent, and sunscreen in a basket on the fridge. There was nothing to kill ants immediately, so I would be going to town again today before I headed home.

I couldn't leave them to rearrange the furniture while I was gone, so killing it is—either them or me.

I did what any intuitive victim would do; I grabbed the spray bottle of Windex. I snuck up to the pods and got to them before they could pass around weapons and receive marching orders from the bigger ants.

I sprayed them down. I know that the ammonia in Windex kills mosquitoes in the air, but I'd never employed the spray-and-pray method on ants. Some were uncles, but I didn't have time to ask them for identification.

It didn't kill them immediately, but I can assure you that it slowed them down enough that I could find my shoes and do an ant dance on their heaving corpses.

I must have killed over a hundred, and I'd never seen those numbers in a daytime raid.

While it was still dark, I reconnoitered the camp from the outside, looking for escapees so I could mark their path of retreat and subsequent return.

Internet advisors find solace in writing that you can always find their path by looking outside for a line of ants coming and going—don't trust them. That's not how it works. They are just reading what other internet advisors wrote before them, regurgitating the pablum so that you feel like you received adequate advice. You didn't.

I knew that the ant-repellent pellets I often sprinkle around the edge of the property were old and had probably lost their luster (read luster as the ability to kill), but waste not, want not. I would buy a fresh bag, probably some spray, and possibly an ant suit to infiltrate the intelligence network—I watched *Hogan's Heroes*.

Woods surround me, trees alive and dead. Deadfalls are common, and there are plenty of places for them to live in harmony with me. I leave them alone when they remain in the hills, and it's unclear why they selected last night for a raid of this magnitude. They probably knew I was alone.

There have been no telltale signs of sawdust, so these rascals came for food and water, showing up just before the rain.

The good news is that I have easy access to all the underpinnings of the camp. Sure, it was easier when I was young, thin, and full of promise, but I can still crawl on my belly to get a command (See quotes from *Patton,* starring George C. Scott, to understand some of these references). This is a war, after all.

Lessons learned:

Windex slows them down, Merrell hikers kill them, and Ellie is absolutely useless, sleeping through all of it until I grab the vacuum to collect the dead.

My Uncle Alan and my father used to joke around together, saying things to each other that made them laugh. They both had infectious laughs and we kids relished being around all my uncles, who were funny men.

Sometime around 1970, while watching a ball game, my dad said to Uncle Alan, "Hey, Alan, can you see that ant over there on the baseboard?"

Alan said, "No, Art, but I can hear him walking."

They both cracked up, laughing in a way that made everyone around them do the same. It's a ridiculous premise, but it's hilarious at the same time.

That came to me this morning as I picked up rugs, couches, tables, and chairs to ensure no hidden squads. I laughed; that's an excellent way to perk up in the morning.

And Dad . . . I can hear them walking.

Oh, How Good It Can Be

Ike's best idea, Interstate 95, is the flowing black ribbon that secures the pine needle follicles of Ms. Maine's center part. The heat from the summer sun made the air pungent, and I partook, pleased, while piloting the private music box that I call Pearl. I headed north.

My vehicles are all painted some shade of blue, so Pearl is always the name—sort of like Air Force One, which is only designated with that moniker when a current president is on board.

My destination didn't matter, but the black coffee did, and it was hot enough so that sipping was impossible until three miles north of Old Town.

Truth be told, without so much as you asking, I'd rather have driven east.

Still, for reasons that are too many to reveal, I went to a friend's cabin for a quick visit, followed by a trip to the Lincoln Walmart to buy six and half quarts of oil for Pearl's next petroleum purge, set for tomorrow at Sammy's house.

I purchased seven for the sake of cleanliness, thus saving the three clerks who oversee the four self-checkout registers from calling in management and a mop.

It's not a big story, but it's my story. I got some sun, took a boat ride where the captain wore a funny hat, and watched some kids fish for nothing in particular while they took turns diving from the deck on one of the most perfect boating days of the year.

I take photos of the road so I can display for those from away that it is possible to drive around Maine and see no one else, sometimes for a very long time. No one would believe that you can drive from here to there running into no other cars. That's why it's hard for so many of us to leave, to go somewhere warm in the winter, and to deal with what you deal with—traffic in spades.

You can get used to this, and I have.

For the record, I have discovered the easiest way to avoid hearing about how the country is divided is to avoid ruminations and excessive lip-flapping about politics at the breakfast counter.

We get overheated because we always try to bring people to our way of thinking. Free advice—you will be unsuccessful.

Talk about the heatwave and the hopes for a good raspberry crop for those pies you've been dreaming about since last August.

Like the rest of you, I relish being informed but turn off the news once I am. What comes after is pontification by pundits posing opinions; by now, you should have your own.

And you can ignore my advice if you like.

Follow me north or east, for that matter; I can take you somewhere where you'll forget how bad it is because you'll see how good it can be.

Superadio II

Both news and song from General Electric Superadio II are Saturday morning staples at the lake. Just as important as the pancakes with blueberries—raspberries when the bears don't get them all first—and slab cut bacon, the Superadio II is the selected instrument of those who are musically limited.

Music from my Canadian disc jockey friends is still clear and comforting. Maine Public Radio brings some valuable information and entertainment into the cabin, and, later in the day, I may even listen to a ballgame.

To be perfectly up front with you, I rarely pay attention to the game. I listen to baseball—in the summer—because of the hushed sound of a crowd in the background, the announcer's voices, and the memories that are dredged up from a place that is masked by the smell of fresh-cut grass, and the taste of vanilla soft-serve ice cream cones during summer evening drives in various blue Chevrolet Impala and Caprice station wagons. They were all a little different, but somehow, they all were exactly the same.

A new car at the Cottons was not often, but it surely was going to be blue, and always a Chevy.

The single speakers in the center of Chevy dashboards are so far away from me now, but I hear them clearly when voltage is added to the GE on the table by the window.

Superadios with the designation of "II" were only available to discerning AM/FM enthusiasts between 1987 and

1991; I am a lucky recipient of such a device, but only because I peruse discarded appliance piles at both town transfer station and neighborhood garage sales. It is the last of the table radios that focused on the life-giving necessity of clear sound from the waning popularity of Amplitude Modulation. FM is available, of course, but the desire for a good AM signal was the reason that this radio exists.

Mine came to me when I was asked to make a run to the dump for lake neighbors. They had no further need of the Superadio II, so I obliged them in their folly with very little forethought. I got rid of the items that were no longer valued, and I kept the jewel of the heap, praying that it would work when plugged into the magic of electricity.

It did.

On late-night trips into the camp, even before starting a fire to drive the hibernating houseflies out of the rafters, I push down the chrome power button with the glee of a kid who is opening his new pencil box upon entry into his fourth-grade classroom. Yes, the feeling is that good.

The radio never disappoints, but its sounds are not welcome to all who might accompany me to this peaceful spot. Very few are afforded the ability to visit the camp with me; it is by design. For if a really good tune needs to be missed for want of excessive and—sometimes—wasteful conversation, it is possible that a visitor may be officially shushed (it's a thing). No offense intended.

There is plenty of time to talk in life but compared to the time we have to just listen, even in the dark, to an old radio, conversation gets far more than its fair share of our time.

I'll miss baseball this summer, probably for different reasons than the true baseball fans who peruse this page. In the end, I believe it awakens the same feelings within all of us.

That's what I am thinking about tonight. I hope your own thoughts are just as peaceful.

Tents, Tarps, Bees, Berries, and Birds

Lying in bed this morning, listening to the raindrops tickle the tarp that topped off the roof, my mind wandered to tents—canvas tents.

The stripping and shingling took longer than the time allotted; it is understandable.

Showers arrived, unmentioned by those tasked with keeping us abreast of weather events in our area. The meteorologist promised that the rain would start around 8:00 p.m. However, it came at two—close, but no cigar.

At first, the shower seemed to be only tiny drops just swinging by to cool us off and make us smile at our misfortune. However, when it became a short-lived deluge, the water migrated into the interior of the camp, dampening all manner of bedsheets covering the third-hand furniture we had collected over the years.

Stalwart and a smidge soaked from the water coming in from above, the Significant One soldiered on, looking for ways to keep the waters at bay.

When you top off a structure with wide, three-quarter-inch thick boards, there are spaces between them, and those widen as the boards shrink over twenty-five years. When unshingled and naked to the world, those crevices take on all the properties of a sieve or colander.

We called it a day and broke out the tarps for the very tippy-top—"the peak"—in man speak.

A couple more hours on a dry day in the future will complete our damp debacle.

Back to tents—this is no different, except there is no seepage. Not yet.

When it poured early this morning, well past the 8:00 p.m. promised by the weather guessers, we were watching for water intrusion.

The good news is that we stayed dry. It made me think of my dad putting up the old canvas Army surplus tent that we used to camp out on various rocky grounds all around Maine and New Hampshire.

I remember trying to find a spot in the ten-by-ten mildewed behemoth where I would remain dry when the dripping started.

Failure is a lesson, and when taught to your kids early, non-success will be nothing but a passing moment to be embraced and released.

Keep that in mind as time passes. A little water in the face never hurts anybody, barring those pesky interrogation techniques seen on television and in films.

I am telling you that we are dry here, and that's good news on a wet day.

The better news is that the raspberry pancakes promised by the keeper-of-the-sheets should be coming along soon.

While we were roofing early, she wandered the old dirt roads above camp, taking photos and collecting wild raspberries.

She claimed it was a good day because she only had to "deal with bees, berries, and birds."

The day came with some fog, too.

Welcome to Maine.